Volkswagen Bay Transporter Restoration Manual

THE STEP-BY-STEP GUIDE TO THE ENTIRE RESTORATION PROCESS

T0377644

First published in April 2014
Reprinted 2020, 2021 (twice) and 2022

A catalogue record for this book is available from the British Library

ISBN 978 0 85733 245 5

Library of Congress catalog card no. 2013934886

Published by J H Haynes & Co. Ltd.
Sparkford, Yeovil, Somerset BA22 7JJ, UK
Tel: 01963 440635
Int. tel: +44 1963 440634
Website: www.haynes.com

Haynes North America, Inc.,
859 Lawrence Drive, Newbury Park,
California 91320, USA

Jurisdictions which have strict emission control laws may consider any modifications to a vehicle to be an infringement of those laws. You are advised to check with the appropriate body or authority whether your proposed modification complies fully with the law. The author and publishers accept no liability in this regard.

While every effort is taken to ensure the accuracy of the information given in this book, no liability can be accepted by the author or publishers for any loss, damage or injury caused by errors in, or omissions from, the information given.

Printed in India.

Acknowledgements
Thanks to Martyn Bulloch for the excellent paint work and to Kev Strange for the help with proof reading and general encouragement. Big thanks also to the staff at VW Heritage for letting me photograph parts and for general help with all things Type 2. Lastly, and most importantly, thanks to Libby for putting up with me while I've been writing, re-writing, editing, annotating and generally taking up good camping time for the last couple of years.

Volkswagen Bay Transporter Restoration Manual

THE STEP-BY-STEP GUIDE TO THE ENTIRE RESTORATION PROCESS

Fletcher Gillett

■ BUYING ■ PROJECT PLANNING ■ STRIPDOWN AND REFIT ■ STRUCTURAL REPAIRS
■ BODYWORK, PREPARATION AND PAINT ■ INTERIOR REFURBISHMENT ■ MECHANICAL OVERHAUL

CONTENTS

CHAPTER 1

INTRODUCTION

Like many of you reading this, I bought my first VW van on a whim. Many years ago, my girlfriend and I went to look at one advertised locally and bought it because we liked the interior layout. We made all the mistakes you should avoid when buying. We did no research, we didn't look at different vans for the sake of comparison, we bought the first van we looked at, and didn't even check the van over thoroughly before buying. We just liked it and bought it. The seller knocked off £50 because the exhaust was blowing ('easy fix') and promised he would get the MOT certificate in the post to me as soon as he found it ('I had it last week!'). Of course it never turned up. We drove away and the realisation dawned on us that we had no idea what we had bought.

We had no idea of the road worthiness of the van and no idea of the condition of the bodywork, apart from the obvious fact that it was blue and white and quite shiny. We knew it was a Volkswagen, but that was about it. It was several days before we realised it didn't need water because it was air-cooled. We learnt very quickly though, and one of the first things we learnt was that they need to be looked after.

As we drove away, the indicators stopped working. It took several months before we noticed they stopped working when it rained, and it took several months more before we realised that water was leaking in under the screen seal and dripping onto the fuse box and indicator relay. Driving back through South London, we noticed more and more people looking at us as the exhaust became progressively louder and louder and finally fell off. When I tried to wind the window down, nothing happened

at first, about 10 minutes later the glass disappeared down inside the door and wouldn't wind back up. At the first MOT, it failed on rusty seat belt mounts and we spent a tenth of the van's original price paying someone to repair it.

I realised that if we wanted to keep the van, I would have to learn to fix it myself.

The VW Transporter is one of the most iconic vehicles on the roads today. Transporter is the name given by VW to five generations of van starting with the 'split screen' in 1950. The Bay is the second generation. When I told people I'd bought my first van, I was amazed how many people had either owned a Bay or had memories involving them, childhood holidays or a gap year trip round Europe. Part of the appeal comes of course from the number that were converted into campers, making them the vehicle of choice for 70s holidays. But they are more than just motorised

caravans and have come to represent the classic image of '70s freedom. **01**

The Bay was VW's successor to the legendary 'split-screen' Transporter, so needed to be a very good vehicle in its own right in order to avoid being eclipsed by its predecessor. VW kept enough of the character of the older van for there to be continuity but changed enough for it to be considered a genuine improvement. The van was bigger, handled better and had lots of technological improvements that made the earlier split-screen seem dated.

Production started in August 1967 and finished in October 1979, although the first model year is 1968. This is the convention for Volkswagen, a model year would start in August of the preceding year and finish in July. Although the Bay remained basically the same throughout its production, there were literally hundreds of changes along the way;

some of these would be introduced at the start of a new model year, others would be phased in during production. It has become custom to divide Bays into 'early' and 'late' vans: '68–'71 are early and '73–'79 are late with '72 vans in the middle known as 'crossovers' partially claimed by both camps. It is a helpful division to follow when referring to Bays, particularly where it applies to some bodywork features, but in reality the evolution of the Bay was gradual and there were changes every year with only the last couple of model years remaining relatively unchanged.

The reason for the changes fall mainly into two categories, safety legislation and cost reduction, with a few others made as genuine improvements, for example moving the filler cap further back so that the tank could be filled with the sliding door open on LHD vans. The most notable changes are the ones associated with the distinctive 'early' and 'late' features.

'Early' vans have small rear lights, wraparound bumpers, a larger engine lid and a removable rear valance behind the bumper. The filler flap is in the middle of the rear quarter. This van has been imported from the States, so the bumpers also have overriders. **02/03**

At the front the indicators are low down, just above the front bumper. The bumper has a step incorporated into it, and the rear vents visible in this shot are smaller and half-moon shaped. **04**

'Late' vans have large rear lights and a fixed rear valance (arrowed). The rear bumper is missing on this van, but

it would be square in profile like the front. The vents are larger and the filler flap has moved to the back of the rear quarter. **05**

In '73 the rounded bumpers were replaced by the square profile Europa-style items and the front bumper was bolted directly to the new deformation panel. The deformation panel was part of the complete change of the front end, designed to absorb energy in the case of an impact. The indicators were moved up the panel to sit next to the air vent and the inner valance was substantially strengthened. The step is incorporated into the arch and cab floor. **06**

This van is a '72, the 'crossover' year. The changes driven by legislation had started and the rear lights became larger, also the removable rear valance disappeared and the new valance was

stronger and welded to the chassis. The front arches became flared to match the rears, which had changed a year earlier. **07**

At the front, it's an early Bay with low indicators. **08**

For the first three years bays had drum brakes all round and the wheels had the 'wide five' stud pattern. In '71 VW introduced disc brakes and an optional servo, and the wheel stud pattern changed to the 'narrow five' style for the rest of production. The rear arch was flared slightly to accommodate the new wheel. There were two different engines used in Bay vans, called the Type 1 **(09)** and Type 4 **(10)** after the vehicles they were first used in. The engine used originally was the Beetle-derived Type 1 engine in single port, 1600cc form. In '71 this changed to twin-port heads. In '72, VW offered the 1700cc Type 4 engine, originally from the 411 car, as an option and the rear vents were changed to channel more air to the larger engine. The Type 4 engine capacity was increased to 1800cc in '74 and again to 2000cc in '76. From '72 onwards the Type 4 was the engine of choice for vans destined for North America, responding better to the increasingly stringent emission regulations than the more basic and lower powered Type 1 unit.

The changes were less noticeable after '73, but there were many of them. This can make buying parts harder so before you buy, particularly anything mechanical, check your van and have your chassis number to hand. In this book I have tried to make note of the model year changes as they come up, but this isn't always possible so sometimes I refer to 'early' or 'late' vans or 'earlier' or 'later'. Checking detail changes is simple in the age of the internet, and the staff at places like VW Heritage or Justkampers will be able to help with identifying parts or locating serial numbers when ordering.

Bay vans were made in several different body styles including an ambulance and a pick-up, but the vast majority of the production was accounted for by Panel Vans, Kombis and Microbuses. Because they provide a holiday and people become sentimentally attached to them, vans converted into campers are more likely to have been looked after and had the necessary money spent on them to keep them going long after most of the unconverted vans have been scrapped. So if you see a Bay plodding gamely along the road, the chances are it will be a campervan.

Check the next chapter for details on how to identify what body type a van is, but if your van is a camper, there's a very good chance it is based on a Kombi or a Panel Van. Considering how iconic the image is of the 'Volkswagen Campervan' it surprises many people when they learn that Volkswagen never actually made a camper – not until very recently anyway. Instead they supplied vans to a legion of independent companies who would convert and sell them under their own name. For example the van featured in this book was converted by a company based in Sidmouth, Devon and imaginatively named 'Devon'. They manufactured and installed the pop top and camping interior and then sold it as a Devon camper rather than a Volkswagen camper. Usually the companies like Devon would use Kombis or Panel Vans for their conversions. Panel Vans are vans with no side windows in the cargo area, used as delivery vans and work horses for a multitude of trades. Camper conversion companies would therefore have to cut windows into the side panels. With this van, windows have been cut into the middle panel and sliding door, but the rear quarter panels have been left without windows. You can recognise these conversions because the side window glass in the cargo area is curved and sits flush with the surrounding metalwork. **11**

Kombis have factory-fitted windows in the cargo area, which are recessed

11

into the bodywork with flat glass. Like Panel Vans they had headliner in the cab area and also doorcards and floor mats, but the cargo area itself was left bare, with no seats or trim, and these were the ideal vans for converters to use. The lack of extras like seats and trim in the cargo area kept the cost of the basic van down but meant that the converters didn't have to fit windows.

A few campers were based on microbuses. Microbuses came with trim in the cargo area including trim panels and headliner, so were sometimes used in the more basic conversions whose spartan camping interiors would leave large areas of metalwork uncovered. This van has trim covering the bulkheads (behind the cab seats), factory interior panels and Microbus-only features like air vents, grab handles and ashtrays in the cargo area. **12/13**

This book isn't meant to replace the workshop manuals and you will need one of those for your van as well. The point of this book is to help you restore your van and it covers the sort of things that you don't find in workshop manuals. When the original manuals were written, the authors had no idea what 30 years of water and salt would

do to the bodywork and mechanical parts of the Bay and no idea about areas of weakness in the design which would take decades to develop into problems. There was also very little coverage of bodywork and I distinctly remember my frustration at trying to work out how panels fitted together from the few black and white pictures included. Bodywork is likely to be the main consideration for most restorations and the majority of this book is taken up with this.

I have tried to avoid needlessly duplicating areas covered by the workshop manuals, but have included the sort of information I would have appreciated when I restored my first van and was new to the world of old Volkswagens, which was mainly how things fitted together and how to fix the rusty bits as cheaply as possible while at the same time making sure I did a good job. This work was carried out in a workshop, but without the use of specialist equipment like jigs and ramps and with a basic collection of tools.

Rebuilding an engine is a book in its own right and can't be properly covered in a manual this size without compromises, and so I'll point you in

the direction of the *VW Transporter 1600 Manual*, book number 0082, also published by Haynes.

Lastly, there are several names for these vehicles: Bus, Kombi, Bulli, Camper, Bay etc. I call them Bays or vans in this book and call vans without side windows panel vans to distinguish them.

CHAPTER 2

BUYING A VAN

Before you go to look at a van, it's a really good idea to spend some time doing some research. As with any classic vehicle, buying a van can be a minefield. At the time of writing, the youngest German bays have been around for just over 33 years. Compared with many vehicles of that age, and younger, they've lasted remarkably well. Nevertheless, rust can be a major issue to consider when buying one and is probably the single most important aspect to bare in mind. I should point out that VW vans are no worse in this regard than any other

vehicle from this period – in fact, they are considerably better than some – but they were designed in the 1960s when anti-corrosion techniques and materials were less advanced. There is also a lot more metal to protect than on most classic vehicles.

Hopefully you've bought this book before buying a van. I've included pictures of how certain sections of bodywork should be. Spend some time familiarising yourself with how these vans should look because it helps when checking for bodges and bad repairs.

GETTING ADVICE

If you've never owned or looked after an older vehicle, it would be worth going along to a local VW club, where you can look at vans and speak to their owners. Or try checking out some of the online communities which cater for classic VWs. A couple of really good ones are thelatebay.com and earlybay.com. Rather than covering all VWs, or all air-cooled VWs, they are only for fans of bays as their names imply. The people on there are helpful and they know that everyone is a 'newbie' at one time, so you don't need to be afraid of asking 'stupid' beginner questions. Another reason for getting to know other people in the 'scene', be it online or in the flesh, is that they may know of good vans for sale or bad vans to avoid. It can be very helpful to have someone who knows their stuff with you when looking at vans and often people are more than happy to help out.

The benefit of taking someone else along really can be invaluable if the person is knowledgable about restorations. Many VW firms and traders including myself have a service which, for a fee, helps people in selecting a van to buy and provides advice at the initial viewing. Even if this service is used several times in order to end up with one good van, in comparison with the expense of a bad purchase and the spiralling costs of an unexpected level of restoration, a viewing fee is negligible and may be the wisest money spent on your van!

Of course this needs to be done by a reputable firm or someone you can trust, but it also means that you will have a ready-made quote for any work that needs to be done, and will greatly help you assess the scale of the project (or parts of it) which you may wish to undertake. This quote can be factored in to the cost of the van and may help to successfully negotiate the price down if it is too high. If you can reliably demonstrate that x hours of welding is needed costing £y then this may give you some bargaining power through the buying process.

Paying a fee for this sort of advice when selecting a project shouldn't be seen as an option only for the technically inexperienced. Even if you are planning and feel capable of a full restoration yourself, another person's view and assessment is a sensible first stage in the process, especially when you consider the time that will be spent in maintaining, driving and camping in your van for the decades to come.

It helps to have clear and realistic expectations of what you want and can afford. Do you want a van you can go camping in straight away, or a van that has had a 'nut and bolt restoration' already? Do you want a complete project, or something in between which is basically usable but needs ongoing work, a 'rolling resto' type van?

The last option is one that lots of people go for, but it's important to realise that if you buy a van that is roadworthy but needs restoration work, you'll probably end up spending more than it would cost you to buy a restored van. It's a false economy to think you'll save money by buying a project rather than a finished van; you won't. But of course you wouldn't have had the enjoyment of working on your own van and the satisfaction of knowing that everything is done properly.

If you want a van as a project, fantastic, hopefully this book will be helpful, but a quick look at ebay or the 'For Sale' sections on forums will show you that people start but don't finish projects. The reason could be money, time, patience, enthusiasm, work space or possibly all of them. It's a good rule of thumb to work out roughly how long you think it will take to restore a van and then double or even treble your estimate. Do you (or your neighbours!) want a van sitting on the drive under a tarpaulin for two or three years?

My intention isn't to put you off. Restoring a van can be a rewarding and enjoyable experience. If you buy a van fully restored, you've got much less chance of getting what you really want, there will always be some sort of compromise. If you restore your own van, you'll be able to choose the bodywork colour, the trim colour and style, seats, carpets, curtains, wheels, even interior layout etc. as you go. You also get to learn how it works and how it is put together. With modern vans like the T5, there's really very little you can do mechanically at home without specialist equipment and knowledge, but a Bay can be fixed by the side of the road (sometimes!).

Like all old vehicles, Bays have certain weak spots where rust tends to start. Consequently, these areas have often been repaired, not always very well. All projects are different, and some vans will be very bad in some areas, but good in others. It's unlikely you'll need to repair everything and the '79 Devon in this book is no different: the chassis was very good, but the front was fairly bad.

It's very difficult to define a point beyond which you can say 'don't buy this van', and it depends on how much of a challenge you want from your project and how confident you feel about doing the work yourself, but if I had to offer a warning on buying a project, I'd say be very careful of buying a van with extensive rot in the roof or chassis. These are a selection of photos that show the common rust spots to look for, and these areas are all covered in greater detail later in the book.

Before any pictures, a quick bit on restorations and viewing vans. Many of the vans I work on have been bought as impulse buys, sometimes because they were a nice colour, or had a cosy-looking interior. I'm in no position to lecture, as you will know from the introduction, but avoid impulse buys, particularly late-night online auction site impulse buys. You'll hear it said that you should never buy a van without looking at it and never buy the first van you see. That's a good way to avoid the danger of the impulse buy even if it does mean you might miss out on a good van. You often see vans that are advertised as 'restored' or 'resprayed'. In an age where everyone has a camera built into their phone, there's no reason for a seller not to have photos showing the work to back up their claim of a 'full restoration'. Ask for proof of any claimed work and parts and if they can't provide it, walk away. You need to be able to see what they've done underneath that new paint.

WHERE TO LOOK FOR RUST

A classic spot for rust and one which is already affecting some of the imported vans from hotter, drier climates, the area round the bottom of the windscreen needs careful attention. Beware of silicone sealer and rust bubbling from under the screen seal. Press the seal hard with your thumb, any crunching noise means rust and holes. If there are holes present, the water will run down the inside of the front panel leaving rust streaks so check under the dash for any signs. **01**

Often related to holes under the screen seal, 73> vans suffer from rust around the deformation panel and the seam at the bottom of the front panel when water gets in. The seam arrowed 'A' is a '73-only feature; on the later years the seam was flat, but regardless of year this area rusts, so check it carefully. **02**

The whole of the front arch can rust. Check around the front of the step where it meets the A pillar and the rear where it meets the B pillar. **03/04**

Front wheel housing/inner front arch. This is a fairly complex area. It should look like this. This is where the front of the sills finish (A). There's also a seam between the bulkhead and B pillar (B). Expect rust here. **05**

It can look like this. This is another classic bodge area, it's time consuming to fix this section properly, so often people opt for the quick fix and simply weld a plate over the rust or even just stuff newspaper or wood in the holes before spraying underseal over it. The outrigger/jacking point has a patch welded over it, but the quality of the welding is awful (C). A length of wood has been rammed into the top hat panel along with some chicken wire to provide support for the fibreglass which has been used to repair this van. **06**

Outer sills on Bays, particularly on the sliding door side are easy to replace, but harder to repair are the sections behind them like the middle sills and the pillars. If you can't see photographic evidence of work on these sections, there's a good chance it hasn't been done. They should look like this with a seam at each end. **07/08**

Look for rust around the rear arch. A proper repair involves removing the old arch. This one had been welded over the top of the old one. This type of work will rust through again in a couple of years. **09**

There are two layers of metal here where the outer arch meets the rear

wheel housing, they are spot-welded together (A). Run your hands along the lip of the arch, it should feel flat. Between the spot-welds you can see where rust has flared the seam. **10**

There should be a seam between the rear quarter and rear corner and it shouldn't be rusty. **11**

Look for bubbling and rust holes around the lower rear corners where they join to the battery tray (A). If the area has had work done, check from inside and underneath for the quality of work. **12**

The bottom of the cab doors rust from the inside out. It can start anywhere along the bottom edge,

but is often worse at point (A). At the moment, it's relatively cheap to get a rust-free imported door, but when the supply runs out, the price will rise. **13**

Sliding doors for RHD vans are already very expensive. The market for RHD buses was obviously smaller than for LHD, so any RHD-specific parts are getting rarer, particularly steering boxes, sliding doors and the door mechanisms. The sliding door should slide easily and should not need to be slammed hard to shut. Rot at the bottom is common and not difficult to fix, but if the door is in very bad condition, replacement will be expensive. Look out for poorly done repair work. The door should sit flush with the B pillar and rear quarter and have even gaps the whole way round.

With the door open, check the condition of the track that the bottom runner sits on. Holes here probably mean you'll need new sills. **14**

In the engine bay, look out for rust under the skirts which sit on top of the chassis legs. **15**

Check the roof and gutters! This is one of the most important areas to look at, particularly around the rear corners. Look out for bad repairs, filler and silicone sealer. Look in the gutters, you should be able to see a continuous line of spot-welds. If they're missing then that area has been repaired, in which case make sure any work has been done properly. When the roof rots as badly as the van in this picture, the only option is to replace the whole thing with the roof from another van. **16**

Once you've had a thorough look at the outside of the van, check inside.

If there are mats under the cab seats, lift them up and check around the seatbelt mount. Grip the belt with both hands and pull to test the integrity of the area. Lift the cab floor mats and carpets. Rust and holes are common here, usually due to the abrasive effects of dirt and stones caught between the metalwork and the mats, combined with water that tends to sit here. In some cases, the rust comes through from underneath. The cab floor sits on top of reinforcing plates between the chassis

rails and water gets trapped between the layers of metal. It's an easy fix if it's just the floor and plate, but remember to check the condition of the chassis rails from under the van. This floor has had a fibreglass repair. **17**

Checking metalwork in the cargo area can be difficult if there's a camping interior fitted, but hopefully you'll be able to get some idea. This section is the other side of the seam between the B pillar and bulkhead, behind the passenger's seat. **18**

It's likely that you won't be able to see the cargo floor. If you can then it's an easy check. The points to look at are the front 5cm or so of the floor which sits on a floor support. Any rust here indicates a fair bit of work. Rust starts from inside the wheel arch and spreads.

This is a seatbelt mount in the rear wheel housing (A). They often rust through and water, sprayed up from the wheels, sits at the rear of the cargo floor. Check for rust coming through where the sills join to the floor (B). **19**

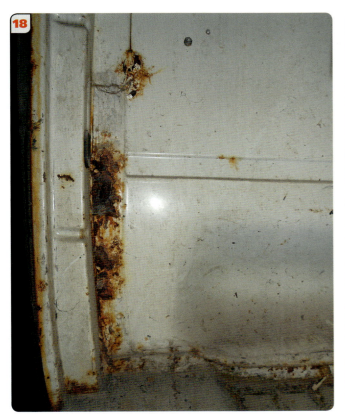

They say you should never buy a vehicle parked in a puddle because it means the seller is trying to stop you looking at the underside. It's vital you have a good look under a van you're thinking of buying, so take a torch and something to lie on. A seriously rotten chassis is a horrible thing to discover, particularly when you've just parted with your hard-earned cash. Beware of thick black underseal, which is often used to hide a multitude of sins and should start alarm bells ringing.

Starting at the front, have a look at the inner valance area. Although the construction is slightly different on early and late bays, they suffer the same problems.

On the '79 the leaking windscreen has caused this. It was hidden under the pedal cover, so if one is fitted, remove it and check along the whole length of the inner valance, particularly around the steering box. Because it's time consuming to remove the 'box to do the job properly, this area often gets 'repaired' with fibreglass and underseal to try to fool the MOT man, and it often works. **20**

Check the front of the chassis legs particularly around the beam and steering box. If this area has had work done, check it's been done well. All chassis repairs should be seam-welded and the weld should be good quality. This van has been parked in a field, and

nothing rots the bottom of a van quite so well as long grass. **21**

Check all the jacking points. If they are patched up badly or swollen inside from rust, they are useless and possibly dangerous if you use them to jack the van up. The VW jack wouldn't fit inside the jacking points on the '79 (A). The bottom of the B pillar had completely corroded away, inside (B) and out (C). **22**

If the inner sills are visible, check their condition as the bottom rusts out. Give them a poke with a screwdriver. **23**

The inner sills and outriggers/jacking points should look like this. **24**

If the van has belly pans, give them

a whack with your fist. If there's lots of rust trapped above, you'll hear it rattling. Although belly pans hide the sills, you can get an idea of their condition by checking the exposed portion at the rear. If this section has been repaired or covered up, the rest of the sills will need work. Here the inner sill (A) can be seen between the rear jacking point (B) and the rear wheel housing (C). That's expanding foam inside the sill (D). **25**

Check the condition of the middle cross-member (A) and the top hat support section (B) above it from the front and back. This support is the front cargo floor support, so if you can't see the cargo floor from inside

the van, this area will give you some clues. Rust starts in the wheel housing and works along the support, and it is time-consuming to fix. **26**

If the van has no belly pans, check the condition of the chassis rails, floor supports and cargo floor. **27**

The area around the rear torsion tube, including the tube itself, should be checked thoroughly. The design was changed for later vans and a strengthening ring (A) was added, making rust here more likely. **28**

Lastly, check the panel the fuel tank sits on. It's hidden behind the gearbox. Extensive rust here is rare, but it's dificult to repair properly.

MECHANICAL

Mechanical parts for the Bay are mostly cheap, readily available and are generally hard wearing, but try to stick with German parts as far as possible as they tend to be better quality than those made in South America. There is also a good supply of secondhand parts to be found through the online forums and at the many annual VW shows. Most parts for the Type 1 engine are relatively cheap, but some of the tinware is not currently available (NCA). The larger sections over the exhaust and behind the fan housing over the gearbox are getting particularly hard to find. Parts for the Type 4 engine are generally more expensive and more parts are NCA, so if the van has a Type 4 engine then check it carefully.

Always consider the condition of the bodywork in preference to the mechanical aspects. A van that needs a new engine but has good bodywork is a better van to buy than one with a reconditioned engine and an MOT but which needs lots of welding. A reconditioned engine can be bought for less than the price of replacing and respraying the front arches, so don't be put off a good van which might have a few mechanical niggles.

Again, you've got to be prepared to get under the van. So before you start or drive it have a look underneath. First impressions count and you may already have some impression from looking at the bodywork. Does the van look like it's been cared for, or just driven and ignored? Are there oil patches underneath where the van has been standing?

Oil leaks are difficult to trace because oil very quickly spreads over the underside of the engine and gearbox when a van is driven. Engine leaks tend to come from the rocker covers, push-rod tubes and the crankshaft seal behind the flywheel. Unless it's just a rocker cover gasket, there's a good chance the engine will need a rebuild. **01/02**

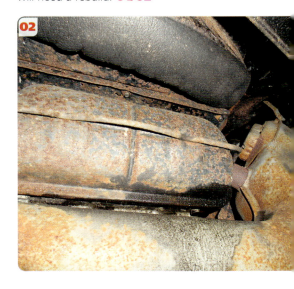

Inside the engine bay, check the condition of the tinware. Apart from being expensive to replace, it is critical for the health of the engine. If parts are missing, particularly the section over the exhaust, the engine might have been running too hot. (A) is the section behind the fan housing. (B) covers the exhaust. Both these parts are hard to come by and expensive if they are beyond repair. **03**

On Type 1 engines grip the crank pulley (A) and pull. If you can feel movement, it's probably too much and the engine needs rebuilding. The fuel lines and hoses should be in good condition with hose clips used. Any leaks are a fire hazard. **04**

The exhaust and heat exchangers should be in good condition. Small holes (A) in the outer casing of heat exchangers can be repaired, but if the exhaust pipe in the middle of the exchanger (B) itself is rotten, new ones are needed. Replacing them is expensive, particularly on Type 4 engines, so check them over thoroughly. **05**

Have a good look at the brake system. Are the pipes in good condition and rust free? The short ones to the front brakes tend to rust more than the others, but it's important to check the less-accessible pipes over the gearbox. The four hoses should be free of cracks or damage. Look for any signs of leaking fluid around the callipers or drums and around any of the unions. **06**

The master cylinder (A) is either found mounted on the front cross-member (B) or on the servo if one is fitted. Any

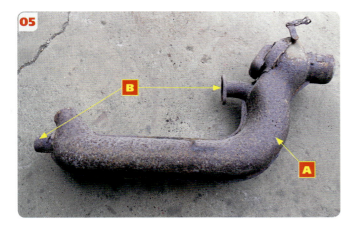

leaks around the master cylinder dust boot (C) mean a new cylinder is needed, and if the dust boot is damaged like this, it's safe to assume the cylinder needs replacing. **07**

Check the front beam carefully, particularly around the bottom sections. Feel around the back of the shock towers; if they are really bad, there will be holes here. There is a reasonably good supply of rot-free beams available, and there are several options for new beams, but they can be very expensive. **08/09**

At the centre of the beam is the swing lever pin housing (A). If the pin seizes, the housing can pull away from the beam. There are a number of grease nipples. If used regularly, grease should ooze out around the torsion arms and swing lever pin housing. Get someone to sit in the van and wobble the wheel from side to side. Check for play in any of the steering joints (B). Note the position of the brake servo (C). **10**

From inside the van, turn the steering wheel through its full range of movement, it should feel smooth.

Assuming the rest of the steering gear is in good condition, check the free play in the steering box. Wobble the wheel; any more than a couple of cm of free movement either way indicates excessive wear. Some adjustment is possible, but if worn out, RHD steering boxes can be hard to find and expensive.

INSIDE AND ON THE ROAD

Inside the van, check the condition of the seats. It became popular to swap the cab seats for replacements from other brands, but original seats are becoming sort after again, particularly for people who like originality. Cab seats (and runners if they're missing) are expensive and hard to come by if they are not there. They can be recovered if needed, but again, this can be quite expensive. **01**

Check the dash pod: does the fuel

gauge work? If it doesn't and the fuel tank sender unit is at fault, it can mean taking the engine out to repair it. It's surprising how quickly it gets annoying if you have to make a note of your mileage to work out when the tank will be empty. It's very likely that a van will have gone right round the clock at least once, so don't be concerned about strangely low mileage readings.

When driving the van have a look in the rear mirror for smoke, particularly with the engine under load. A bit of smoke on start-up is OK, but it should quickly clear. Due to the length of the gear change linkage, gear selection can take some getting used to. This isn't necessarily a big problem, as the linkage is relatively easy to fix, but if the van jumps out of gear under load, or you notice whining, the gearbox will need reconditioning. When pulling away, the clutch action should feel smooth, if it judders and jumps it can indicate oil on the clutch drive plate from the gearbox, or more likely the engine. Either will need attention.

These vans can't be driven like a sports car, but considering their weight and dimensions they feel sure-footed if everything is in good order. If you've only ever driven modern cars you might be in for a surprise: they won't accelerate or stop as quickly, so remember that when driving. If the van tends to wander as the road camber

changes, suspect worn ball joints or steering linkage. The brakes work well if adjusted properly, even if the van has drums all round. Test them out when safe to do so. The van should brake in a straight line. If it pulls to one side, the brakes need an overhaul.

Push the heater levers down as you are driving. If the heat exchangers and pipework are in good order, you should get a reasonable blast from the vents, certainly enough to clear a foggy windscreen on a cold day. If you get an oily smell coming through the vents, it means there is an oil leak and engine oil is running over the exchangers, if you get a smoky exhaust smell, it can mean the heat exchangers have holes inside – wind the windows down! If you get a petrol smell in the cab, particularly after cornering, something's wrong with the fuel system, often perished hoses, requiring urgent attention.

There are too many camping interiors available to cover them, but it's worth bearing in mind that missing parts or damaged sections can be expensive to replace, so check everything's there and that it works. Westfalia interiors are hard wearing but very popular so expect to pay a premium for any parts you need. The '79 in this book originally had the 'Moonraker' interior, but it was long gone when I bought the van. Although the design and layout of the interior was excellent and the culmination of

decades of R&D by Devon, the company swapped from using plywood to chipboard for its units halfway through the 70s, which soaked up moisture like a sponge and unfortunately the bottoms of many of the interiors have turned to mush.

Check the condition of the pop-top if present. All are prone to cracks in the fibreglass and ripped canvas/vinyl, which can be easily overlooked when buying a van but can be expensive to repair. On vans with bigger pop-tops like the Devon in this book or the Viking conversions, the metal work of the roof can take a real hammering. With the pop top up, check down the sides for rust. The hinge has rusted and pulled away from the metal roof. To fix this the pop-top needs to be removed (see chapter 9). **02**

These struts help lift the pop-top and hold it in place once it's up. The design changes depending on the roof, but usually involves either springs or hydraulic struts, so check they work properly. **03**

These are old vehicles, and the chances of buying a van that needs no work is very unlikely, and in my opinion, boring. But if you're equipped with a bit of knowledge and you know for example that it will be expensive to replace the pop-top canvas or the fuel tank sender unit, or the spice rack for your Westfalia, you can use that to negotiate the price.

VEHICLE IDENTITY

It goes without saying that you should carefully check the identity of any van you consider buying. Thankfully, ringing (the process of swapping a vehicle's identity) is less common on Bays than on vehicles with a separate chassis, but it can happen. The reason for ringing a van can be as relatively harmless as wanting to use an older van's identity to gain tax-exempt status, but less harmless, and unfortunately on the increase, is the practice of using another van's identity to hide a stolen van. Almost all Bays have identification numbers in triplicate, so check they are all there and that the numbers match.

■ The VIN (Vehicle Identification Number) or Chassis plate. This is riveted to the bulkhead behind the right-hand seat. **01**

■ In the engine bay. '72–'79 vans, the number is stamped into the metal on the raised section of the skirt on the left-hand side

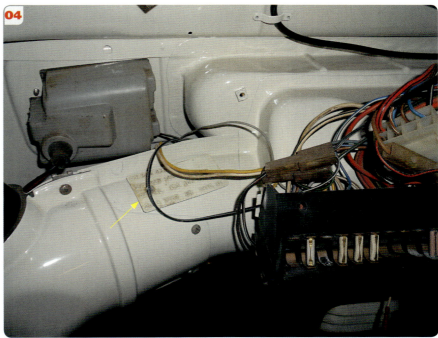

of the engine bay. On '68–'71 vans the VIN number is a bit more tricky to find. It's on the right-hand side near the bottom of the air filter. **02**

■ On the M plate. It's riveted to the bulkhead behind the left-hand seat on '68–'76 vans and on the air-box on '77–'79 vans. **03/04**

DECODING THE M PLATE

Ordnung Muss Sein! (There must be order!)

It's worth having a look at the M plate here. VW, with their Teutonic love of efficiency and order, designed a system for listing all the details of an individual van, including VIN, paint colour, optional extras and so on. There are literally hundreds of variables, so for help with yours, I'll point you in the direction of VW-MPlate.com. On this van, the options show:

■ VIN number, minus the '23' at the beginning (A).
■ Optional extras: 172 is the code for radial tyres, 506 for brake servo, A51 is a group code for vans destined for the UK, it shows the van has headlights for RHD countries, a sticker about seatbelts and double the amount of fuel put in at the factory for driving on and off boats etc. (B).

■ Paint colour and interior: the paint colour here is two groups of two, so two for the colour of the top of the van, two for the bottom. Sage Green and Pastel White in this case. The last two digits is the code for the interior, Canyon Brown Leatherette (C).
■ Destination code for export: Ramsgate, England (D).

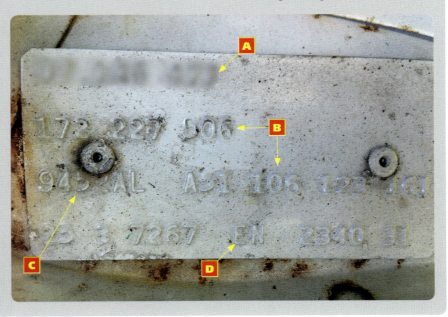

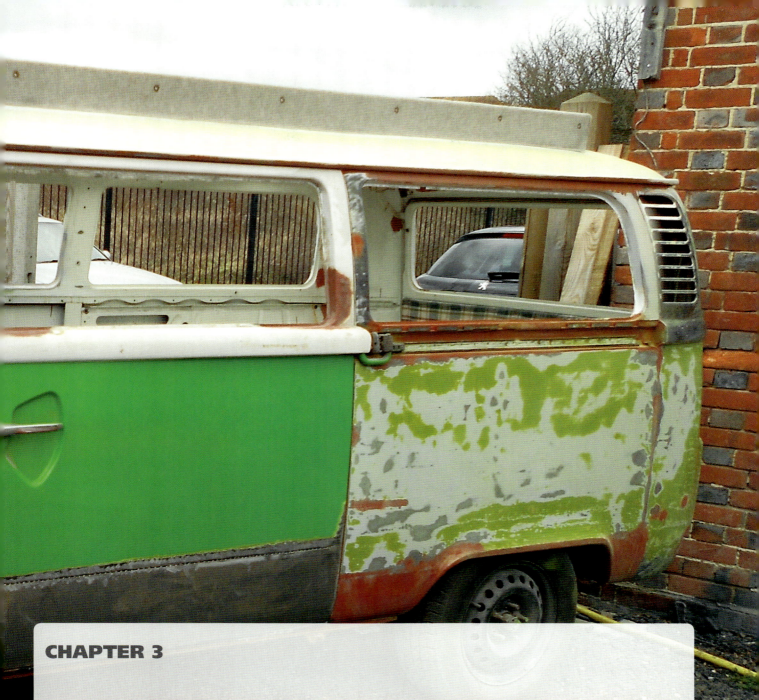

CHAPTER 3

STARTING THE PROJECT

Before starting your project, sit down and plan it out. Things to consider are timescales, costs and the working area. Ask anyone who's restored a van before and they will say that everything takes longer than you expect. As mentioned earlier, it's a good idea to double your time estimate, but this should only be a rough guide. I find it works best to not set myself deadlines when working on a project, unexpected problems can arise and nowhere is this truer than when restoring old vans. Your manual might say, 'undo and remove x', which on a new vehicle might take 30 minutes, but on a rusty 40-year-old vehicle might take half a day. You might allocate one day of time to replace a front arch, but when you remove it you find you need another couple of days to sort out the surrounding metalwork. It quickly becomes dispiriting and I find I rush jobs I'd rather take more time on.

I mention all this because when I restored my first van, I had the use of a friend's workshop for three months, which I naively assumed would be more than enough time. Three months came and went and I had to move the van into a field under a tarpaulin to complete the work because the workshop was needed. The tarp blew off and ripped no matter how well I tied it down and everything got wet. Luckily I'd finished the underneath of the van. Avoid this sort of situation if you can!

Although the timescales are harder to control, the costs can be worked out fairly accurately at the outset after a good check over the whole van. It's usually safe to assume the worst, so if a panel looks like it might need replacing, it probably will. Sit down and work out the prices of all the panels. Some suppliers offer a 'restoration reduction' and this can save quite a bit of money if you buy everything at once. Remember to include things like door trim and seals and also consumables like paint, filler, masking tape, grinding discs, grease, oil and so on.

If you have access to a work area with a roof, you're lucky, but in reality a lot of DIY restorers will be working on their driveways and will have to deal with whatever the weather throws at them. A good cover is vital, as is a safe working area. Obviously, you can't use your use axle stands in a field, but also be careful using them on tarmac, they will sink in, particularly in hot weather. If your drive is tarmac, use some thick metal plates under the axle stands to spread the load.

Another mistake I made was to attempt my first restoration in one go. After the demoralising realisation that I wasn't going to get it all done in three weeks, I plugged away for another four or five months (part time of course), before getting bored and losing interest for half a year. I then came back to it and by the time I finished, the van had been off the road for nearly two years. With hindsight I should have split the job up into smaller sections. I could have then used the van for a summer season,

which would have kept the motivation levels up. Restorations don't always neatly divide up, due to the way the panels overlap and the work needed on your van might be decided by the dictates of the MOT man, but it's worth considering.

When it comes to starting the work, I always like to get the underneath done first, then work my way up. This is for several reasons: it's the least pleasant area of the van to work on, even if you've got the luxury of a body roller or a ramp. It's dirty, noisy work cutting and grinding the underneath of a van. If you've got access to a pressure washer, get as much of the loose dirt and rust off first. Pressure washers are not usually a good idea as they force water into bearings, seams and box sections, but you're just about to restore it so you may as well. It is also likely to be the biggest and most time-consuming section of the welding stage of any restoration and once it is done, you know that the other sections will be easier. Lastly, the construction of the Bay window means that sections such as the inner sills and outriggers really need to be done before you attempt the overlying panels.

The order I follow is: chassis, cargo floor, supports, sills and outriggers, front, front arches, rear arches, inner valance, rear corners/battery trays, rear outer valance, then anything else like

window apertures, roof repairs and door repairs.

When it comes to stripping the van, the amount you remove will of course depend on the extent of the work you plan to undertake. Strip down and reassembly is covered in Chapter 12, but at this stage the most important thing to say is that it is essential to label and bag everything as you take it apart, and even photograph more complex sections to help you remember how it all went together. It takes a little longer to do things this way, but I can't overemphasise how much time and stress you will save yourself in the long run by doing this. If you remove, for example, the screws that hold the dash to the A pillars and put them in the glove box, you'll feel certain that you know where they go, but after a couple of years when it comes to reassembly and you've got a glove box full of nuts, bolts and screws, you'll have absolutely no idea where any of it belonged. So label and bag everything as you remove it. **01**

If you have a camping interior, you'll need to remove and store it somewhere safe and dry, along with the curtains, cushions, seats and interior trim panels. Put fabrics and cushions in sealed plastic bags for added protection. Any welding to the underside of the cargo floor area carries the risk of starting a fire if you've got a wooden floor in

place, so it is important that this is removed as well. Even if you're not replacing sections which necessitate the removal of the interior, you'll need access to the insides of the rear arches, door pillars, etc.

If your van is inside, you may as well remove all the glass at the start. If the van is outside, you may want to keep the glass in for as long as possible to keep the weather out. If you do, cover both sides of the glass with cardboard to protect it from grinding sparks. This rear window has been ruined by someone grinding near the unprotected glass. The red hot metal melts into the surface of the glass and then rusts. You can remove the specks of metal using a razor blade so that the surface of the glass doesn't feel like sandpaper, but you can't remove the marks left in the glass without extensive polishing. Incidentally, the same principal applies to the surface of your eye, apart from the polishing bit, and it's a needle not a razor blade they use to remove the speck, but more of that in the next section. **02**

HEALTH AND SAFETY

You'll be in contact with some potentially dangerous substances while working on your van, so it's important to wear the correct protection.

Always wear a mask. I use one with a carbon filter to remove the vapours given off during welding. It also gives your face some protection as it's fairly sturdy. I sometimes use a lightweight dust mask when rubbing down filler or doing mechanical stuff, but always some sort of mask. Even when you're not grinding or rubbing down filler or doing something that actively generates dust, there will be dust around the van from previous work. Although it was phased out 20 years ago, there is also the possibility of asbestos from the brake and clutch linings so whenever you work on these areas, make sure you've got your mask on and spray brake cleaner or light oil over the area to trap the particles. You'll also need one for paint spraying if you plan to do it yourself, but for that you will need at least a mask like this one from 3M. If you're planning to spray 2-pack paint, you must use an air-fed mask and it needs to be sprayed in a booth with a filtration system, so it's not suitable for a DIY job at home. As its name suggests, 2-pack paint has two parts, the paint and the hardener which contains isocyanate, it gets in to your body through your lungs, skin and even eyes and can literally be lethal. **01**

Goggles are an absolute must. It's worth spending a bit on goggles. These ones cost about twice the price of the cheapest sort, but the lenses on the cheap ones scratch easily and you'll find yourself having to lift the goggles to avoid the haze of scratches. Apart from sparks and grit from angle grinding, they also protect your eyes from rust and dirt when working under the van. I had to go to hospital when I got a spark stuck on my cornea. I'd had goggles on, but it flew up under the gap between the goggles and my cheek. At the hospital you rest your head in a cradle to keep it still while a doctor with a steady hand picks the metal off the front of your eyeball with a hypodermic needle. Not an experience I'm eager to repeat. **02**

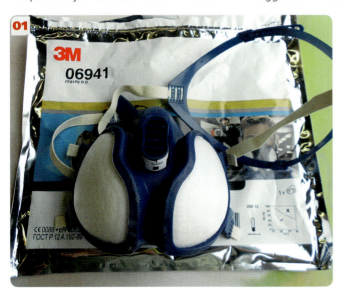

Used engine oil is carcinogenic, so avoid getting it on your skin. Gloves like these protect your hands from oil, paint, and all the other nasties you might come into contact with. They are cheap and offer a surprising amount of protection from the cuts and scratches you inevitably get from working on rusty old vans. Your local household waste disposal site will take used oil and also dead batteries. **03**

Welding arc gives off ultraviolet light which burns skin, so make sure none is exposed. Always wear a welding mask. It's sometimes tempting to not bother with a mask for tacking and even plug-welding, but even with your eyes shut you run the risk of arc eye and I wouldn't like to think what a blob of weld would do to your eyelid if it landed on it. Arc eye is sunburn of the cornea and it feels like your eyes are full of grit. Again, one to avoid. For welding, some people use gauntlets, but I prefer tig gloves. They're not quite as heavy duty, but they allow a degree of dexterity you can't manage with the thicker gauntlets and they are useful when handling metal and glass. If you're working under the van, a leather apron is a worthwhile investment. Blobs of weld will quickly burn through clothes and even flame-retardant overalls, so if you have no option but to be in a position directly under the area you're welding, the apron comes in handy. You can also use them

to cover things like tyres or dashboards if you are welding nearby and don't want to risk damaging them. Other things to have are ear defenders; angle grinders are very noisy, particularly in an enclosed area like a wheel housing. A kneeling pad is good for saving your knees and comfortable for lying on underneath the van. Steel-toe-capped boots may seem like overkill, but you only need to drop a brake disc on your foot to be in plaster for months, so err on the side of caution.

Store anything flammable away from the area you are working in. This includes the interior and seats, gas bottles and cannisters, and also things like chemicals, thinners, brake fluid, petrol, the petrol tank itself and batteries, which give off an explosive gas that can be ignited by grinding sparks. Remember that grinding sparks can be thrown a considerable distance, and when you are concentrating on grinding you may not be aware of what's going on around you. Keep a couple of buckets of water around when you're welding and a fire extinguisher. Have a cooling down time at the end of each welding session before you leave the van, 30–60 minutes with no welding or grinding. I try to plan some non-welding/grinding jobs or just spend the time clearing up.

This is easier said than done and I don't always do this, but it helps to clear everything away at the end of each day, even if you know you are going to use the same tools tomorrow. You're much less likely to have an accident if you don't have tools and bits of old metal and tins of filler lying around on the floor. Plus you're less likely to waste half an hour looking for that 10mm spanner that's hidden under rubbish. Clear up any metal fragments as you go and put them in a sturdy box to avoid the risk of punctures to tyres or cuts to yourself when they stick in clothes. **04**

01

TOOLS

It is worth buying some good quality tools before you start work. The amount of time and stress it will save you far outweighs the cost, so buy the best you can afford. Cheap tools will slip or break and round off nuts and bolts. Not only is this dangerous, it's also extremely annoying.

I bought this set to keep in my van a few years ago but found it so convenient I rarely use my other tools now. It can be a bit expensive to buy sets like this, but you will spend more buying everything separately. It has a mix of ¼- and 3/8-drive, with deep and shallow sockets, and the larger 3/8 ones are six sided. The spanners cover 10–19mm. A tool set, a range of screwdrivers, pump pliers, circlip pliers, wire cutters, a set of punches, a couple of hammers and some chisels will be enough for most of the mechanical jobs you'll find on your van. **01**

These are invaluable. (A) is a selection of mole grips/panel grips. You'll need quite a few of these in different shapes and sizes. (B) are tin snips, you'll find you need to use these all the time for trimming down panels so don't buy the cheapest type as they blunt quickly. (C) are pump pliers. **02**

Also very handy is a joggler/joddler.

Mine is hand operated, but air-powered versions are available. It also has a rotatable head with a 6mm hole punch, which makes panel prep much quicker. It can punch through body panel thickness's up to about 1.2mm.

There are a few items you will need but less often, so it might be worth renting or borrowing rather than buying. You'll need a 46mm socket and breaker bar for the rear hub nuts. ½ or 3/8 drive

breaker bars will break, so use ¾ or 1-inch drive. You will also need a scaffold pipe or similar for extra leverage. A set of impact sockets are handy, if you have use of an impact wrench. You'll need a puller for removing the drop arm on the steering box and probably for the camber nut on the top ball joints on the front beam. You might also need a joint separator for the ball joints.

Bay window vans are too high to

02   A   B   C

use with standard car axle stands if you're planning to spend lots of time under the van, so invest in some decent ones. Often they are marketed for use on 4WD vehicles. Likewise, you need a decent trolley jack. The red one shown should be the minimum size you buy, the smaller yellow one is capable of lifting a van, but the maximum saddle height is so low that the van wheels barely leave the ground. It is useful for removing engines though. Always jack the van up safely and avoid using the chassis. Position the axle stands under the front and rear torsion tubes, or if you are removing the front beam, use the point at which the front outriggers and chassis meet. **03/04/05**

You'll need a drill, of course, and spot-weld drills. There are a couple of different options. The ones with the separate crown and sprung centre point are not worth using in my opinion. The crown shatters easily and you need to centre punch anything you want to drill or the centre point will drift, this doubles the time it takes to get anything done. The other type of drill bits are quicker to use and longer lasting, they come in 6mm and 8mm. You'll need a few blocks of wood, they come in handy for various jobs and should always be used behind panels if you are drilling holes. Drill bits are blunted in seconds if you drill through into stone. **06**

Apart from the welder, the angle grinder is probably the single most useful tool for restorations. Buy a good one as they take a lot of abuse. Better quality ones also tend to have thinner

bodies which makes holding them a bit more comfortable. It can be tempting to remove the guard for better access in certain situations, but avoid doing this if you possibly can. A cutting blade will cut a finger off in a moment and when you are concentrating on your work, it's easy to move your hands near to the disc without noticing. Always hold the grinder with both hands, particularly when using wire wheels or cup brushes as they can catch and kick back. These cutting discs are 1mm, and you can also buy 0.75mm. They cause much less heat than the thicker variety and make removing old panels a joy. They are a bit expensive, but work out cheaper if you buy them by the box rather than individually. Likewise, buy grinding discs by the box. The flap discs are really helpful for grinding down welds to get a smooth finish. Like sandpaper, they come in different grades. Use the wire wheel and cup brushes for removing surface rust and paint. **07**

You will need a compressor if you plan to spray the van yourself. See chapter 11 for more information regarding capacity and output. **08**

Buy a good quality welder, check online for a welding forum or find

your local specialist shop for advice. A MIG machine is the easiest route into welding for the beginner. It is worth renting a bottle of gas for the period of your restoration from BOC, the small disposable bottles last very little time and you will use dozens while restoring a van. If you are new

to welding, spend some time online or consider buying a book for advice on techniques and machine setup, or sign up for an evening class – often run at technical colleges. Online forums usually have a 'newbie' section, with advice on machines and 'how-to' videos on welding techniques. **09**

WELDING TECHNIQUES, PANELS AND PANEL PREP

You will find you have to repeat the same prep process each time you fit a new panel, so for the sake of brevity and to avoid repetition, I won't repeat this information at every stage of the welding process unless there is something extra to include.

Wherever possible, buy genuine panels and parts for your van. Reproduction (repro) panels are generally poorer quality, although there are some exceptions, and the extra expense of genuine parts will be easily offset by the time you save fitting them. In some cases there will be no option and the only panels available are repro quality, for example front arches for '68–'71 vans. Most panels come in a transit primer to stop corrosion. On most panels it can be left on, on some it needs to be removed and new paint applied. It's simple to check, if the paint flakes off easily when scraped with a coin, it needs to be removed. If it doesn't, it is fine to leave on the panel, although it will still need to be covered with more paint.

There are replacement panels for nearly the whole van, but you will also need some sheet steel, which you can buy from your local metal fabricators. Body panels on Bay vans are about 1mm thick, some sections like floors are slightly thicker,

1.2–1.5mm and the thicker sections like the chassis are 2mm, so get a few sheets for different applications.

Bare steel needs to be painted or it quickly begins to rust and the moisture present in the air is enough to start the process. Some sections of the van are inaccessible, like the back of the rear arches, the inside of the chassis and seams, or the inside of the sills, so any painted protection you want to apply needs to be done before you fit the panels. When VW had finished welding the body-shell, it was dipped in an immersion tank filled with an anti-rust coating, which covered all the hidden surfaces and seeped between the panels and seams. You can spray Waxoyl into some of these areas for extra protection, but it's a good idea to use weld-through primer on areas around any welding and paint the areas that won't get welded first, then Waxoyl everything later for added peace of mind.

Weld-through primer isn't as tough as other paints, so use it sparingly. Remove as little of the transit primer as you need and spray some weld-through primer on the bare metal, Scotch-Brite the rest of the primer before painting. Paint and prep is covered in Chapter 11, but these few pictures show you what you need to know for the welding section.

Firstly, Scotch-Brite the transit primer. **01**

Punch holes in the panel return if necessary. In this case it allows the arch here to be plug-welded to the rear corner. I'm using a joddler/joggler with a rotatable head that incorporates a hole punch here, but you can use a drill although this is more time-consuming. Then spray a couple of coats of weld-through primer on to the areas of bare metal. **02/03**

When you remove the transit primer, use a cup brush or wire wheel or flap disc. A grinding disc is too coarse and will leave deep scratches in the metal, which will act as the starting point for rust.

There are a few different panel joining techniques:

■ Two panels are clamped together and either plug-welded or spot-welded. Almost all the panels on the Bay van were originally joined together using a spot-welder. There are

also a few places that are joined with seam welds for extra strength. Unless you have access to a spot-welder, you will need to plug or seam weld new panels into place with a MIG welder. A plug weld replicates a spot weld without using a spot welder: a hole is drilled in one panel which is then usually clamped against another panel before the hole is filled with weld, joining the two parts together. In this photo you can see the factory spot welds joining the strengthener to the body of the outrigger (A), you can also see the plug welds I've used to join the outrigger to the top-hat support and the chassis (B). The repair patch on the chassis has been seam-welded (C). **04**

■ The new panel overlaps the old panel slightly. The outer panels of the van should never be continuously seam welded, particularly the large flat ones like the rear arch, as this generates too much heat and the consequent expanding and shrinking of the metal causes lots of distortion. Instead weld in one-second bursts. If you are welding the rear arch for example, start in the middle and then move to one side, then the other, then back to the middle, so that each area has time to cool down before you return to it. Gradually fill the gaps between the welds. You can either completely fill the gaps making a continuous line of weld or leave areas of a centimetre or so, which minimises heat distortion. **05**

■ The panels are overlapped again, but one of the panels has had a step pressed into it using a joggler. This keeps the two panels flush with one another. This technique is only really applicable on the large side panels when joining a new rear arch or sliding-door repair, or possibly on the front panel, and unless you have an air joggler, it is time-consuming pressing the step in by hand. If you do decide to join your repairs this way, remember that if, for example, you tuck a new rear arch under the old rear quarter, with the joggle in the new panel, you will find that any Waxoyl or paint on the inside of the old panel will melt and run down and contaminate the weld, so put the step in the old panel. In this diagram (A) is the old panel, (B) is the new panel, (C) is the point to weld. Any contaminants will run down away from the weld. **06**

■ Butt weld: the two panels have a small (1mm) gap between one another, which is filled with weld, joining the two panels together. To make sure the panels are perfectly in line, you can use these intergrip clamps. **07**

Remember that using an angle grinder on metal generates lots of heat and you can cause almost as much distortion by aggressively grinding welds down as you can with the welding torch, so take your time.

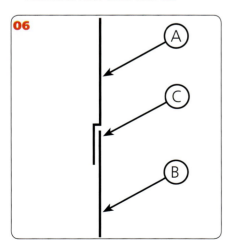

CHAPTER 4

CHASSIS AND UNDERSIDE

The middle section of the van comprises the inner, middle and outer sills, the cargo floor and supports, two cross-members, jacking points and outriggers, the bottom of the B and C pillars and the chassis. As you might expect it's quite a complex area and, generally, isolated repairs on individual sections are unlikely because firstly, the sections are joined together in a way that makes this difficult; and secondly, if rust has taken hold, it's likely it'll be found in several sections. So if you can see that you'll need to repair the outer sills you'll probably need to repair or replace the middle and inner sills as well. Similarly, if you need to repair holes in the front of the cargo floor then you'll need to replace the top-hat support beneath it.

Personally, I like to tackle this area first when restoring a van. It's the dirtiest area to repair with lots of potential for welding burns and rust/mud/underseal in your eyes, but it's rewarding to know its all done and that the bits you don't see are solid.

You may find your van has belly pans covering the sections between the jacking points. These were optional extras which could be ordered from the factory. Camper companies often ordered them to add extra strength to the van structure before cutting a massive hole in the roof for a pop top. They consist of three panels: a large centre one that sits between the chassis rails, and two smaller sections either

side which cover the space between the chassis and the sills. Belly pans can be a mixed blessing. They protect the support sections and underneath of the cargo floor, but they were welded in place by Volkswagen and rust often starts at the welds when moisture gets trapped between the pans and the section they're welded to. Initially Volkswagen welded them onto the flat of the chassis rails and cross-members, but around 1974, they started bolting the middle pan on rather than welding it. **01**

If your van has belly pans, it is impossible to know exactly what you will find underneath until you take them off, but you can get a few clues. If there's rust flaring where the pans are welded

to the van, there will almost certainly be holes underneath. Extra patches welded to the belly pans mean someone's covered up some rust, probably to please the MOT man. They won't have repaired the rot underneath because you need to remove the whole belly pan to do the job properly.

This van has had belly pans at one time. This happens when somebody cuts the belly pans off but doesn't take the time to grind the last bit way from the chassis rails. You can see the remains of the belly pan with rust bulging underneath. **02**

You'll need to assess the condition of the underneath of your van and decide what needs replacing.

On the '79 I managed to save the N/S rear outrigger/jacking point and part of the inner sill, but in reality it would have been quicker to cut them out and replace them. The sills on the Bay Transporter are made up of three separate sections: the inner, middle and outer. The inner and middle run from above the jacking point at the rear of the front inner arch to the front rear wheel housing. On the sliding-door side the middle sill has a door track incorporated into it on which the sliding door bottom roller sits. Later vans have no middle sill on the non-sliding-door side.

To remove the old sills, you need to drill out the spot welds joining them to the cargo floor. There are two lines of spot welds. (A) inner sill spot welds, (B), middle sill spot welds. **03**

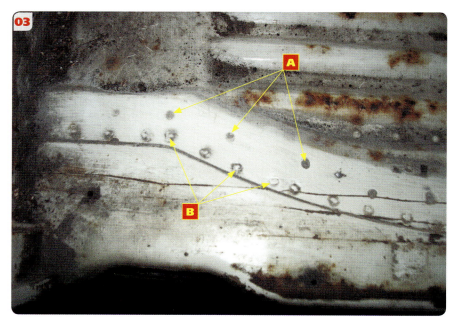

On the sliding-door side only remove the inner sill spot welds, not the middle sill ones! More about this later. Once you've drilled out the spot welds, it is easier to cut the inner sill into sections until all that remains is a small bit spot welded to the ends of the top hat, which you can then grind away.

If you also need to replace the outrigger/jacking points – and there's a good chance you will – the quickest way is to remove the sills, top-hat support and outriggers at the same time. Cut close to the chassis and the inner sill, then above the seam between the outrigger and top hat. Do the same inside the front wheel housing but don't cut too high above the seam or you'll risk cutting through the front of the cargo floor. The whole lot will usually come free after a few whacks with a hammer.

With the outriggers in place it is much harder to get to the inner sill, particularly if you're working on the sliding-door side, as you need to keep the middle sill as intact as possible. It's also difficult to remove the outriggers without damaging the top-hat support above them so you'll need to decide how much needs to be removed. Often the extent of the rust decides this for you. In this photo there are patches on top of patches. If I took the time to slowly remove it all, I'd find the top-hat support and outriggers would be rotten, so it is quicker to cut it all out. **04**

The top-hat support under the front of the cargo floor is a horrible section to replace on a bay. They almost always need

replacing although you can sometimes get away with just replacing the sections above the outriggers. The part above the cross-member is time consuming and fiddly to cut out due to the lack of access, which makes it very difficult to get an angle grinder into position. If you have access to items like an air saw or cut-off tool, they will help. This photo from later in the sequence shows the whole of the area. (A) inner sills, (B) outriggers/jacking points, (C) front floor support/top hat, (D) cross-member. **05**

It's particularly difficult to remove the spot welds between the top hat and cross-member, but often the cross-member needs attention so it's easier to cut it out at the same time, which makes access to the top hat slightly better. Cut out the cross-member in sections, but be very careful not to damage the cable-guide tubes, the wiring loom or the brake pipe. I find it helps to use zip-ties to tie the loose guide tubes to one side for better access.

This is the heater tube diverter. It allows warm air heading for the front of the van to be channelled up into the cargo floor area. If it is very rusty, it may be better to remove it and extend the heater tube to the crossmember. **06**

The tube that carries the wiring loom usually rusts out after water gets between the loom and tube. Grind away the spots of weld that hold it to the crossmembers, then very carefully cut it away. You may be able to do this with a cutting blade on an angle grinder, but it's really easy to damage the loom. I used a pair of tin snips to cut it open. **07**

You can replace the tube, but it means disconnecting the wiring loom and pulling it back through the cross-members, which is a lot of extra work, so I zip-tie it to the inside of the chassis.

The front of the top hat (A) is overlapped by and tacked to this panel (B). **08**

If you need to replace the cargo floor at the same time, it's much, much easier to do all this from above, although you'll still need to get under the van occasionally. That said, don't rush to replace your floor to avoid doing everything from under the van. The best quality floor sections are from VW Brazil and are still noticeably thinner steel than the original German floors. If you only need to repair a

09

few sections on your cargo floor, do this in preference to replacing a full floor.

To illustrate this process, I've included some photo's from a '74 which needed a new floor and repairs to everything else.

It's a good idea to buy the new floor before you start cutting the old one out. There are a couple of options for new cargo floors, a cheaper repro floor and a better offering from VW Brazil. If your van is RHD with the sliding door on the left, you'll need to modify the floor.

Both the genuine and repro cargo floor panels are for LHD vans and therefore the section of the floor near the sliding door is different, but because the shape of the inner sill is the same on both sides, regardless of whether it's a LHD or RHD van, the corresponding pressing in the floor is the same on both sides along its whole length (A) so you can modify the LHD panel to fit RHD vans. **09**

The cargo floor is spot welded to each of the supports at the bottom of each corrugation as well as to the inner and middle sills, so that adds up to a lot of spot welds to drill out! You also need to make sure you don't drill right through the supports because it's easier to drill and plug weld the

new floor from above so you don't want extra holes in the supports. Because of this, it's easier to do the following: draw a line through the middle of the spot welds using a rule. This shows the correct location of the floor supports beneath the floor. **10**

After a good look underneath the van to check for potential sections that could be damaged, cut a few cm either side of the marker line, taking particular care as you cut through the floor above the gear shift guide tube, which sits just below the centre of the floor. Then grind each of the spot welds. This doesn't take as long as you'd think, certainly not as long as drilling them all, and I find that I don't need to grind them all the way through to the supports, just enough to thin and weaken the metal. **11**

It's then possible to pull the strip away from the supports. **12**

The plates in the floor are for securing bench seats in the rear of kombis and microbuses. Unless you plan to put factory bench seats in, you don't need them. **13**

The last support was so rotten it ripped out with the floor. It was full of newspaper and underseal. From a reference in the paper, it was possible to tell it was a fairly recent bodge. **14**

Once the floor is out, take the opportunity to do everything you can from above that's a struggle to do from below. On this van I scraped the underseal off the chassis and repaired it, replaced the sills, cross-members, outriggers and floor supports, repaired the heater duct, cleaned everything and painted most of it before replacing the floor.

The floor is out, but everything else is still in place. I've cleaned up the tops of the floor supports I'm going to save. **15**

The cross-members look OK from underneath, but someone has welded new ones over the rusty old ones. **16**

As mentioned above, it is best to cut the cross-member and top hat out in sections, this helps with access. It's much easier with the floor out, but the principle is the same. Here I've cut most of the top hat (A) and cross-member (B) away, leaving the tricky front overlapped section (C) in place which I can now cut out from behind, roughly along the dotted line (D). **17**

FLOOR SUPPORTS

The floor supports change slightly depending on the year of the van. Sometimes they are a mixture of I beams and top hats, sometimes just top-hats. They are all spot-welded to the cargo floor. The front four supports have the gear-shift-rod guide tube running through them (A), so to replace them you need to either cut the support through the middle and re-weld once in place (B), or remove the guide tube, which is tacked to each of the supports. I prefer not to disturb the guide tube if possible and in this case it was only the front support which had the guide tube passing through it and which needed replacing. If you are replacing all the supports, you may be better removing the guide tube. **01**

The two supports at the rear don't have the guide tube mounted in them, so leave them in one piece. Disconnect the gear shift coupling (A) just in front of the gearbox and the joint just behind the front beam (not visible here). You can then move the rod (B) towards the front of the van allowing the supports to be slipped into place. **02**

The front support is always a top hat, and is narrower than the other supports because it sits between the front part of the inner sills. The available top-hat supports come in one length and need

to be cut down if used at the front. When you're shortening the top hat, you can either measure the length of the front support before cutting everything out, or offer the new inner sill up and clamp it into place against the remaining floor supports. You can then measure the distance from the gear-shift-rod guide tube to the inner sill and cut each end of the support down accordingly. Remember to leave extra to make new tabs (A) to weld to the sills! **03**

From inside the van, you can see where I've tacked it to the chassis (A). As with all these bits, it's a good idea to not weld anything in completely until you've trial-fitted the outriggers and sills. This will do for the moment. **04**

This support has seat belt mounts in it and a strengthener which welds the support to the chassis. Make sure you replace it if you intend to use the floor mounts. **05**

Mark the place where the supports and cross-member sit against the chassis using a scribe or pen, when it comes to refitting, make sure the new support is parallel to the one next to it by measuring the distance between them at each end. **06**

This Y-shaped heater duct is welded to the rear cross-member and tacked to the lip at the rear of the cargo floor, which is probably why it has rusted through here. Repair it and paint it before putting the floor in. **07**

CROSS-MEMBERS

There are three cross-members, the front one is under the cab floor, the middle and rear ones are in line with the jacking points. The rear cross-member used here is a genuine VW Brazil item, but needs extensive modification, mainly because there's no hole for the heater duct to pass through and the guide tube cut-outs are in the wrong place. Start by cutting a hole for the heater duct to fit into, mark it out by scratching the primer. **01**

You can then push it into roughly the right place, which will allow you to make accurate marks for the guide tubes (A). **02**

Once you have cut the necessary slots, it's ready to fit. **03**

The middle cross-member is a repro one and has the holes in the correct place, but unless you want to spend the time removing the wiring loom to go through the hole, you'll need to cut a slot in it. When you do any welding near to where the loom passes through the cross-members, make sure you weld in short bursts and let it cool down or you'll risk melting the loom. The same applies to the brake line: cut a small slot in the cross-member if you don't want to disconnect it (A). You will also need to protect the loom and brake pipe from damage at the points where they pass through the cross-members. Use rubber grommets. **04**

When you are ready to weld everything in finally, remember to tack the guide tubes to the cross-members and supports. They only need to be tacked in place to stop them moving, don't risk blowing through the guide tube as any damage to the inside of the tube could fray the cables. The heater ducts need a run of weld on both sides of the cross-members to stop them moving. **05**

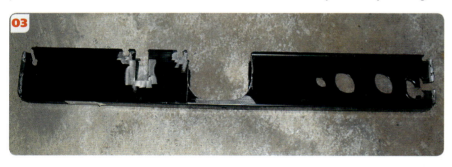

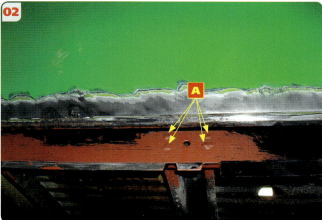

INNER SILLS

The '79 needed sills, outriggers, jacking points and the front top-hat support. I used the Just Kampers top hat here, which is a really good panel. **01**

I clamped the sill into place and then made marks where the supports meet it. I then drilled holes in the sill so that I could plug-weld the sill to the support (A). You don't have to do this, it just makes a neater looking 'factory' repair without a spot welder because you cant see the welds. Doing this on the sliding-door side is harder because the middle sill/sliding door track is in the way. However, it's still possible if you cut the middle sill away up to the track as described in the middle sill section. What I intended to do at this point, but forgot, was to weld a few captive nuts into the inside of the inner sill so I could bolt new belly pans on rather than weld them. I could have then cleaned and painted them before fitting the outer sill. Oh well. **02**

The join between the sill and support looks a bit neater from underneath (A). **03**

When fitting, the same applies to both sides, push the inner sill up against the cargo floor. The pressing in the floor corresponds with the cut out in the sill, so you can't position the sill too far forwards or backwards. Clamp the sill in place and then position the outriggers to check everything fits together before welding it in. **04**

Fitting sills on a van with the cargo floor in place is relatively easy because you

have the fixed points of the cargo floor and usually most of the floor supports remaining to locate the new sill. On a van like the '74 without a cargo floor, there's slightly more opportunity to get it wrong.

The top of the new sill (A) should be level with the sliding door step (B) as the cargo floor sits on top of both. Again, this pressing (C) can be used as a reference point to ensure the sill is not too far back or forward. **05**

The other side won't have the sliding

door step (unless your van's a twin slider), and in this picture you can see there is not a lot of metal left to use for reference points, so fit the sliding-door side first, then measure the gap between the top of the support and sill and use that measurement to locate the non-sliding-door-side sill. As with the '79, I'm trial fitting the sill and outriggers at the same time to double check everything is in the correct place. Hold in position with clamps (A) before welding. **06**

The position of the front of the sill is difficult to get wrong because it sits on top of the front of the outrigger. The top-hat support sits on the chassis rail, the outrigger/jacking point is welded to it, then the sill sits on the jacking point, but it's still worth taking the time to measure and check everything as you go, particularly if you are using separate outriggers and jacking points that need welding together. Lots of clamps come in handy here! **07**

OUTRIGGERS

There are three pairs of outriggers on the Bay, and the front and middle set incorporate jacking points. The rear pair are just outriggers and VW replaced them on later vans with a strengthener (A). **01**

Sometimes the replacement jacking points and outriggers come separately, in which case you need to weld them together. These are Autocraft replacements and they are really good quality. However, they do come covered in an anti-corrosion oil, which needs to be removed before you weld them on.

Here I've degreased them and coated them with weld-through primer to give a bit of added protection. **02**

You can plug-weld the new outriggers to the chassis and supports and inner sill, but you should always seam weld this part (A) to the cross-member. **03**

Another advantage of working on a van with the cargo floor removed is that when it comes to plug-welding everything together you can do it from above, so rather than drill holes in the outriggers to weld to the support, drill the holes in the support instead. The obvious exception is the front middle section, which joins to the cross-member and can only be done from underneath.

Notice that there are gaps in the metal on the outriggers, cross-members and supports. Trial fit everything

together with clamps and mark the correct places to put holes to avoid punching through an area which won't be covered. Here I have scratched crosses into the primer of the floor support to line up with the cross-member beneath, although I must have jogged the support slightly while taking the photo because they don't quite line up. **04**

Once you are happy with the position of the support, cross-member and outrigger, weld them in. **05**

The '74 has the proper outrigger at the rear of the cargo floor rather than a strengthener like the '79. It sits directly below the last floor support. **06**

With everything in place and welded in, paint as much as you can before the floor goes in. Anything not covered now will have to be done from under the van later. **07**

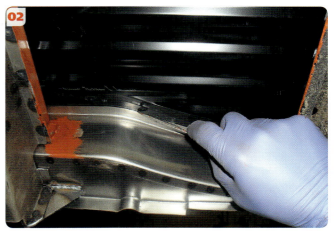

FITTING THE CARGO FLOOR

Trial fit the floor. The right side goes in first. This side had holes for the seat belt mounts located in the floor support, which made lining the floor up easier. The left side didn't. When you're certain the floor half is in the correct place, mark the position of the supports from underneath the van so you know where to drill holes for plug welding. **01**

At the same time, mark a line showing the position of the top of the inner sill against the floor. **02**

When the floor is turned over, the line is clearly visible. **03**

Make sure you don't get confused and drill holes in the wrong place. So when you flip the cargo floor over to see the lines that correspond with the floor supports, be sure to drill holes in the part of the floor corrugations that will be against the support. Likewise,

drill the holes for plug welding to the inner sill on the correct side of the line you've drawn. This may sound stupid, but it's easily done. It's also worth going over the underside of the floor with Scotch-Brite to help with paint adhesion later on. I remembered to do this side, but not the other side so I had to do it from underneath. **04**

Remember to drill holes for the returns where the floor meets the bulkhead, the wheel housings and the side panel. Weld the right half into place. You won't need clamps to hold the floor to the supports, your weight will be enough. On a RHD van, you then need to make up a piece that extends out from the edge of the floor to the side panel. **05**

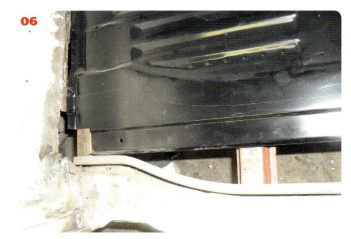

The left side is basically the same, but you need to trim the panel down first. With the new floor lying next to the step you can see the mark I've made to cut the floor to fit the shape of the step and inner sill. You also need to drill two lines of holes, one for the inner sill and one for the step/middle sill. **06**

This van needed repairs to the rear-wheel housing and the panel between the housings so rather than carefully drill the spot-welds to remove the floor, I cut the housing and floor out together to save time. The wheel housing looked okay, but was mostly made of fibreglass. It would have been better to replace the whole housing, but there were none available at the time, so I repaired it. The wheel housings are complex items to repair, particularly around the edge that joins to the rear quarter/arch. This one needed a repair in several places, here you can see the edge that meets the outer arch/quarter panel (A), the repaired section (B), the strengthener (C), and the rust/fibreglass of the housing inside the van (D). **07**

With all the fibreglass and rust cut out, there's not much left. **08**

The new section welded in. The cargo floor is plug-welded to it at the bottom (A). The strengthener needs to be reattached to the housing (B). **09**

Inside the wheel arch. **10**

The '79 is more typical, with localised rot starting around the seat-belt mount. **11**

Cut it out and be sure to seam seal the new section you weld in from underneath. The seat-belt mount itself isn't reusable, but as I'm not sure about the layout of the interior at this stage, I'll leave it out until I know where everything will go. Overlap the repair for extra strength if you plan to put a seat belt mount there. **12**

The panel between the housings (A) is NCA. It joins to the cargo floor, bends up under panel (B), and finishes as the section the fuel tank sits on. Usually, it's possible to do localised repairs, but in this case it was too far gone. Someone had previously made a repair section but had left the old panel in place under the new one. **13**

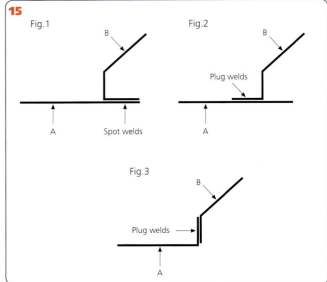

All cut out. **14**

Originally, this panel bent back on itself and was spot welded to the back of the cargo floor, forming a lip that you can see from under the van. It's very inaccessible, hidden behind the torsion beam and the Y-shaped heater duct. Rather than try to plug-weld it from under the van, I made the new panel with a different profile and plug-welded it from inside the van. Fig.1 shows the original design with the inaccessible lip. Fig.2 shows how I did it. It retains the original look, because the back of the cargo floor still forms the lip, but it needs to be seam sealed from underneath, which isn't easy. Fig.3 shows another way that involves putting a 90-degree bend in the back of the cargo floor and plug welding to the new panel again from inside the van, which is probably the easiest way to repair it. (A) is the cargo floor, (B) is the panel between the housings. **15**

Once in place it looks good, but I was unable to replicate the pressings, so made it from slightly thicker metal than standard to give extra strength. You can see the plug welds joining it to the cargo floor. **16**

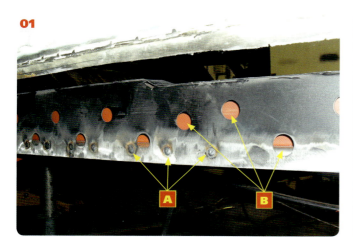

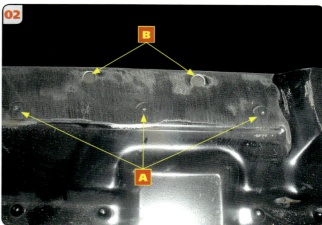

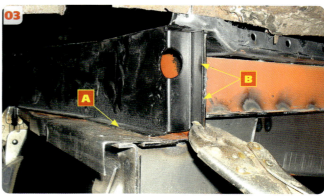

MIDDLE SILLS

Volkswagen stopped fitting the middle sill on the non-sliding-door side in '75 or '76, so the '79 doesn't have one. On the '74 it was fitted once I'd welded the floor in place. It needs to be plug-welded to the inner sill (A). It's worth painting the inside of the inner sill before fitting the middle (B). **01**

From inside the van, you can see the ground-down plug-welds for the inner sill (A) and the holes for the middle sill with the sill pressed up against the floor (B). Alternate them for extra strength. **02**

Weld the middle sill to the horizontal surface at the front of the inner sill (A). The front edge lines up with the front of the inner sill and they should be plug-welded together (B). **03**

You may remember I said earlier not to drill out the spot welds for the middle sill on the sliding door side. That's because no matter how badly corroded the original is, you're better off repairing it rather than replacing it with a repro one. The original sliding-door track is curved, and the lower sliding-door runner follows this curve as the door closes. The sliding-door track on the repro middle sill panel doesn't have that curve. Instead of the curve, the panel has straight lines, so the door jolts as it follows the panel.

You can get a good idea of what goes where from this picture taken part way through cutting the rot out on the '79. Inner sill with the underneath cut away (A), middle sill (B), underneath of the sliding door track, note the curve (C), B-pillar cut back to just below the cargo-floor level (D). **04**

The '74 is a bit worse and here you can see the previous repairs. The van has had a replacement inner sill, with the

sticker still attached (A), but the middle sill has been left unrepaired (B). **05**

Cut as little away as possible and repair it rather than replace it. When I repair this area, typically I find I end up cutting the middle sill back to just below the track and replacing that section, and repairing the front of the track around the B-pillar. Less often, I might need to replace the whole track and the section below. If you need to make any repairs to the track itself, take measurements first and tack repairs into place, but before welding them in permanently remove the bottom runner from the sliding door and check it moves up and down the track freely. There's not much room for error here, if the track is slightly too high the runner will stick, slightly too low and the guide wheel won't be in its channel and the door will drop out. On the '74, with the new inner sill in place, the middle sill is cut back to the track (A) and the front section of the track is completely removed (B). **06**

When replacing the lower section of the sill, clean the grease off the track or it will melt when you start welding and run down between the track and sill, contaminating the weld. Make up some sections to replace the lower portion of the middle sill and plug-weld it to the inner sill and seam-weld to the remains of the middle sill/track. The holes in the original middle sill are to allow Waxoyl to get inside the outer sill (I think!), so either replicate the holes, or leave gaps in the replacement sections. **07**

The track is welded to the inside of the B-pillar. Here I've repaired the B-pillar first, then made a section to replace the front part of the track. This can then be joined to the remains of the original track.**08**

To do this I used the edge of an O/S inner sill I hadn't fitted to get the correct curve. **09**

It's worth mentioning here the importance of correctly repairing the bottom of the B and C pillars. They often get ignored, and on the '74 new outer sills had been fitted and the pillars and middle sills had been left. On the '79 they weren't as bad but still needed repair. They are important because they transfer the weight of the van up into the pillars when the jacking points are used. If they aren't in place, the sills and floor supports take the weight on their own. The '79 needed fewer repairs to the track, but more to the B pillar.

Cut back until you get to good metal. **10**

The view from inside the van. **11**

Make up a couple of sections to replace the inside of the B-pillar. **12**

You can then use the B-pillar outer repair panel. Use as little as you need and butt weld (A) to the old outer (B). This panel replaces the bottom outer section and can be used on both sides. In most cases, this part combined with some sections fabricated from sheet metal will be enough to repair the B-pillar. However, a panel that replaces the inner pillar up to the wheel housing is available in addition to the outer repair if it is really bad. **13**

Close the B-pillar in with a section of curved metal. You can get a repair panel for this section but the fit isn't great, so

replicate it unless you want to for the sake of originality. The repair section from the previous photo welds to the B-pillar and bulkhead. The repaired inner B-pillar has been ground down to look neater (D). **15**

Finally, close the section below the bulge. If you're lucky, the rot will be confined to the easily repairable flat sections of the bulkhead, but often the bulge needs attention. You can get a repair panel with this bulge pressed into it, but it still requires a lot of modification. The middle section is fairly easy to repair, the end isn't. Cut away as little as you can and if you have access to panel beating hammers and a sand bag, it's possible to make up small curved sections without serious panel beating skills. **16**

The '79 needed a repair to just below the bulge, but you might need to make one that goes further up, like this. **17**

The bottom of the pillars are particularly important on vans like the '79 without the middle sill. On the

make your own using tin snips. Slide the repair (A) under the outer part of the B-pillar (B). The inner sill should extend out through this panel; weld the repair to the sill (C). **14**

From inside the van, you can see how the whole repaired section looks. The seam here is often the starting point for rust (A). VW seam sealed this area from the outside and once the sealer hardens and cracks water quickly gets in. The seam joins the bulkhead (B) to the B-pillar (C) and isn't a strength requirement, it's just a handy way of joining two panels in a factory with a spot welder, so you don't need to

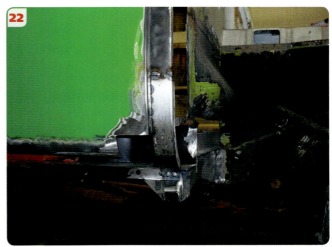

bottom of the C-pillar I've used thicker 2mm plate, welded between the jacking point and the pillar as it comes through the cargo floor, then, to stop that flexing, I've replicated the curve at the bottom of the pillar. Check that the shape of this curve won't foul the inside of the rear arch. **18**

The B-pillar on the non-sliding-door side is slightly more difficult to repair because it sits against the middle panel. The original outer B-pillar is formed differently to the repair section. Here you can see that it continues into this seam (A), whereas the repair panel stops after about 1cm. There's a line of spot-welds joining the B-pillar to the middle/side panel (B). Cut the

B-pillar back as far as these spot-welds but no further. If you cut further back, you'll need to rejoin the pillar and middle panel. If you don't cut back to here, the new section will sit on top of the remains of the old and they won't line up properly. **19**

Trim the new outer down to fit the cut-back area. **20**

Spend a bit of time making sure it fits neatly. Look down the side of the van and check it sits flush with the middle panel. When you weld it in, do it gradually. If you put too much heat into the panel, you'll find the pillar will twist slightly. **21**

From the front the new section sits tight against the middle panel and in line with the original part of the B-pillar. **22**

Make sure you remove all of the old sill from the underneath of the track (A). The masking tape is to cover the holes in the middle sill to stop grinding dust getting into the inner sill. **01**

Drill holes in the sliding door track or grind a series of notches. These can then be filled as you plug weld the sill to the track. **02**

Plug-weld the outer sill to the track and middle sill. **03/04**

On the non-sliding-door side, the sill is joined to the middle panel and the two are spot-welded together from behind. Obviously, you can't get to the rear of the seam because of the middle and inner sills. Like the sliding-door side, this sill is available as a genuine or repro offering, and like the sliding-door sills, they will fit a LHD or RHD van. If you use this outer sill, you'll need to weld along the seam between it and the middle panel, then grind back the welds to make it look neat.

OUTER SILLS

For the sliding-door side, you have the option of repro or genuine VW Brazil sills. Although the pressing on the repro panel is good, it doesn't have the lip that holds the door seal in the channel, so you'll need to glue it in. The genuine sill is only a few quid more and well worth it. Unfortunately, there where none available when I repaired the '79, so I used the repro item.

More likely though, is that you'll need to use this panel. If the outer sill needs replacing, the chances are that the rust will have spread up into the middle panel. As the area around the seam is a fairly complex shape to replicate, this panel is an excellent replacement because the seam is pressed into one sheet of metal, so your repair will look original once fitted, but you know you'll have no more problems with the seam rusting. **05**

The panel extends to just above the cargo floor and overlaps the B- and C-pillars so the sides need to be trimmed down. Take your time and get it correct, trim the same amount from each end to ensure the seam is the same width either side. **06**

On the '79 I've cut the repair panel down to just below the floor line so that the repair isn't visible inside the van. I've overlapped the panel slightly although it may have worked just as well joggling the new panel and tucking it under the middle panel. I've butt-welded for 3 or 4cm at either side to help lose the join. **07**

Once it's got some primer on it, you can see better how this works. The panel is overlapped for most of it's length (A), and butt-welded at each end (B). The edges are welded to the B-pillar (C) and rear arch, then the seam is carefully ground in. It then needs a very thin skim of filler to get the shape correct around the welds. **08**

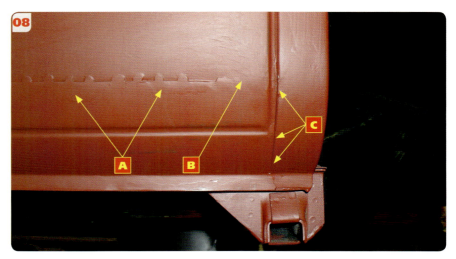

CHASSIS REPAIRS

There are several repair sections available for the chassis. The front outer legs from just in front of the beam to the inner valance, the rear legs on '72> vans as they pass through the engine bay, and a middle section for the area below the cargo floor. If you need to replace large sections, remember that the structural strength of the Bay is not reliant solely on the

chassis. The middle section in particular relies on the integrity of the connecting sections for its strength, so don't for example cut the cargo floor, the sills, the pillars and outriggers away, then decide to replace the chassis leg because there will be hardly any strength left in the shell, particularly if you've got a camper with a hole cut in the roof.

It's quite likely that rather than replacing whole sections, you'll need to make repairs. On the '74, this damage is the result of water trapped between the strengthener welded into the chassis near the middle cross-member and from the remains of the belly pans, which were welded to the chassis bottom at this point. There's also a hole which was behind the outrigger. **01**

Use 2mm steel for all chassis repairs. It's much harder to work than the usual body stuff but it needs to be this thick for strength. All chassis repairs need to be seam-welded. You could butt-weld this bit to make an invisible repair, but it's quicker and stronger to do it like this. Remember to repair the strengthener if needed and to weld it to the new repair. Cut back to solid metal and seam-weld new sections in. **02**

The other side had a hole behind the outrigger, but the bottom of the chassis was okay, so all that was needed was the rot cut out and a plate welded in. **03/04/05**

The worst area was behind the rear outriggers. This was hidden behind the thick underseal covering the bottom of the van. Someone has previously tacked a bad repair over part of the rot (A) before covering the rest with a new outrigger. You need to remove the handbrake-cable guide tube (B) to fix this properly, which is probably why they didn't bother. First you need to remove the handbrake cable – you can follow this in your workshop manual, or check the mechanical section later in this book. The guide tube is tacked to the cross-member, the torsion beam and to the other guide tubes. Measure how far it extends beyond the middle cross-member and the point at which it passes through the chassis (C) so it goes back in the same place, then carefully cut away the tacks, and draw it out. **06**

With the cable guide tube removed, the rotten part can then be cut out and replaced. **07**

Drill a hole and elongate it to allow the guide tube to pass through. Once back in position, run the cable back through to check it doesn't stick before tacking the guide tube into place. **08**

CHAPTER 5

FRONT PANEL

The front end of your van is almost certain to need some kind of attention, and it's an area that suffers from several problems. It is the favoured location for the spare wheel in many camper conversions and as the front panel is just a single skin of metal in most places, the slightest of knocks against the spare will dent the front. It is also prone to rot under the screen seal, which often goes unnoticed or ignored for long periods of time. The problem often starts with a perished screen seal. This allows water to get in and sit in the screen aperture, which acts as a water trap. It makes good economic sense to take the windscreen out every two or three years to change the seal and check the condition of the panel.

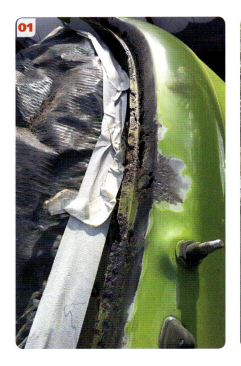

This rust has been caused by someone cutting a cracked windscreen out and scoring the paint underneath, the score line ran round the whole of the aperture, but serious rust had started at the bottom where water collected. **01**

If the screen aperture has rusted through above the air vent, any water that gets in will collect between the front panel and the inner screen surround where they join the air-box (A). If the holes are in the bottom corners, the water will get between the front panel and the A-pillars (B). Water collects at the bottom of the front panel on the inside (C). On late bays, the seam joining the front to the inner valance will rust. **02**

There are quite a few options for repairing the front, and you'll need to decide which best suits your van. This is another section of the Bay where it is preferable to repair rather than replace if possible because the original front panel is better quality than the repro skin.

However, if the front needs repairs in several areas, like the '71 later in this section, it may be better to replace the whole front.

The available front panel is for '73> vans, although with modification, it can fit a '68–'72 van with low indicators.

These three sections make up the bottom of the window aperture behind the seal, although often the rust will have spread out from under the seal into the bulge area, so additional repair sections may have to be made. **03**

If you decide to use the windscreen surround repair sections, they will need a fair bit of fettling to fit correctly. Butt-weld, or underlap the repair sections rather than overlaying them. The van in these pictures needed the windscreen surround repaired and the entire width of the lower panel above the deformation panel. Restorers will often argue that it is quicker and cheaper to replace the whole front skin rather than repair several sections of the same panel, and often it is, but on this van the panel was fine above the air-box and around the A-pillars, so I decided to repair and keep most of the original panel.

The lower section had been filled and primed but not repaired, the area

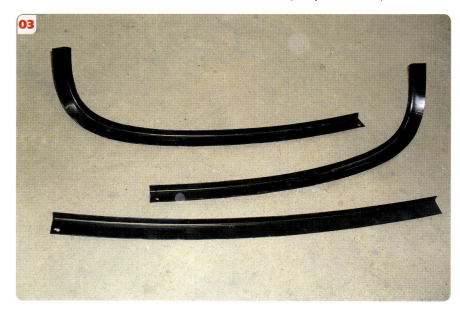

around the screen had rust creeping out from under the seal. **04**

If you can see rust around the windscreen with the screen and seal in place, it will be worse underneath. **05**

The screen surround repair sections laid in place. **06**

Cut away the rust including any that has spread into the bulge. **07**

Once repaired, grind the welds down. **08**

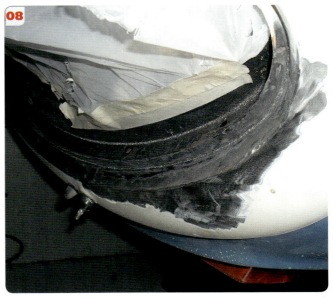

The lower section had holes along its entire length. **09**

Cut the lower section out carefully, and note the two tabs that help locate the front panel – don't cut through them (A). The top of the inner valance is visible; paint it before welding in the new section. **10**

I used the bottom 10cm of a replacement front skin as a repair section. **11**

Finished! **12**

If you decide to replace the entire front skin, it is easiest to cut the old panel out in several sections. It's the same principle regardless of whether you're replacing the front on an early or late van, but if it is an early van then save these sections if they are in good condition because you can use them on the new panel. I used the early indicator sections but decided to use the blanking panels you can

buy instead of the cuts from the old panel. **13/14**

Before you start cutting anything out, it's worth taking measurements of the window aperture. With 73> vans, it's difficult to get the new panel in the wrong place because it sits on the inner valance, which fixes its position. However, there's a little more scope for error with an early Bay, so it's best to be safe and take measurements. I've included measurements, but take some anyway for your own peace of mind. The measurements arrowed (A) are both 54cm, the measurement arrowed (B) is 57cm. **15**

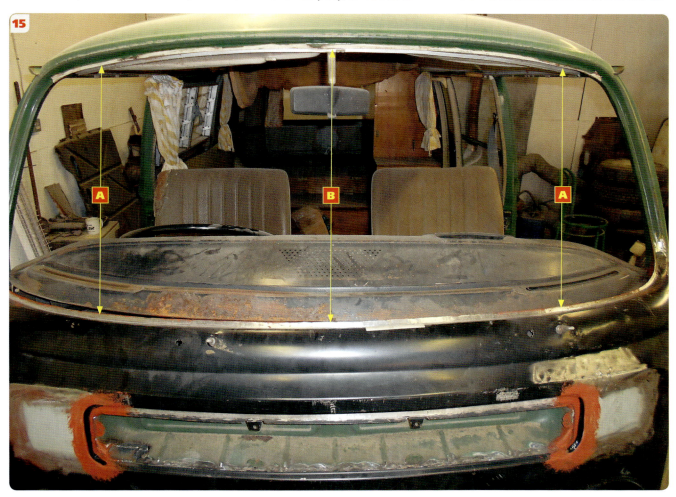

Measurement (B) is taken centrally, use the hole for the rear view mirror as a reference point. Measurements (A) are in line with ends of the grill aperture, which are painted red here. The distances are between the lip of the aperture (1), rather than the recess (2). **16**

Cut the front away in sections. Take care not to cut the wiring loom, which comes up into the cab behind the front panel, and also the locating tabs. Once you've cut most of the panel away, it's much easier to remove the last bits. **17/18**

The front panel folds round the A-pillar. Although it isn't spot-welded at this point, it is tacked into place. **19**

The easiest way to remove it is to carefully grind down the edge, making sure not to damage the A-pillar. If you grind carefully, you get a point when the metal turns blue as it thins just before you grind right through. Watch for this and you'll avoid grinding into the A-pillar. The thin orange line (A) is the A-pillar with the remains of the front panel on either side. **20**

Once the front panel is cut away you can see the inner windscreen surround panel. Water that gets through holes in the front panel sits above the air-box and causes this rust. Note the rust-coloured streaks down the panel. **21**

If you find that the inner surround panel is rusty – and it often is – you can replace the whole panel or just the ends. Once it had been cleaned up, it was obvious this one needed replacing. **22**

If your dash is still in place, you'll need to move it back to cut the old panel out. Refer to chapter 12 but instead of removing the whole dash pod, you only need to disconnect the speedo cable. This will give you enough movement to pull the dash away from the A-pillars and make the repairs. Take measurements! I've measured from the edge of the lip in

the centre and also from the edges of the air vent to ensure the new panel won't be crooked. I also made marks on the inside of the A-pillar to show the point the top of the panel reached.

Note how far the new panel extends up the A-pillar. If you cut away at an angle, you can avoid disturbing the section of the A-pillar above the bulge (A). The ends of the inner surround panel are welded to the A-pillar (B) from inside the cab, but if the dash is in place they can be removed from this side. **23**

You'll need to keep the bits that the dash screws to and weld them

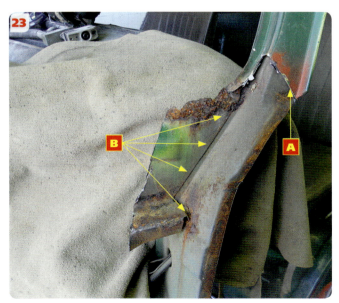

to the new panel. There are two separate sections. On this van they were in good-enough condition to keep, but you may need to repair or remake them. The pressing on the new inner surround is good and matches the original panel well, so positioning the dash mounts is straightforward. **24/25**

Later vans had smaller tabs, which were part of the inner surround instead. The VW Brazil panel has no mounts so you'll have to make some up if the originals are too far gone. **26**

Prep the A-pillars and air-box before welding the new inner surround panel into place. **27/28**

With the dash pulled back (A), you can just about get enough clearance to

weld the inner surround panel to the A-pillars. **29**

Water ends up collecting here if it gets in and this panel sits directly on top of the inner valance, note the spot-welds (A). If it rusts through, it can be an MOT issue when near to the steering box. All that is normally needed is a few repairs using sheet steel, but the whole panel is available from VW Brazil. It is the same panel that the front of the cab floor is spot-welded to and it holds the washer bottle, so I'll call it the washer bottle panel. On this '71 the inner valance has rusted through along the lower lip, but the washer bottle panel isn't too bad. Some of the water must have pooled here, but most ran down the inside of the panel and rusted the bottom of the valance. **30**

INNER VALANCE AND A-PILLAR REPAIRS

If you need to replace the front panel, there's a good chance that you'll need to do some work on the inner valance and A-pillars. **01**

Rust is rarely isolated to one panel; here the inner valance (A), A-pillar (B) and step (C) all need attention. **02**

A-pillars

You can buy complete A-pillars from the gutter to the bottom, which you could use if your pillars are completely rotten, or in the case of crash damage. In most cases, you're better repairing your own and normally they only rot as far up as

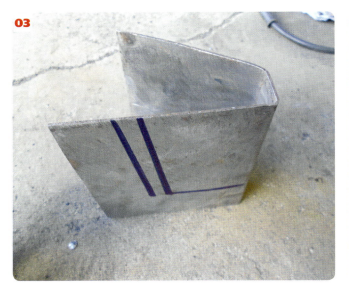

the first hinge. It helps to leave as much of the original metal in place as possible while you make up a template. The pillar bends back slightly just below the lower hinge and then tapers down as it nears the bottom, so it can be tricky making up repair sections.

The A-pillar is two sections made of different thicknesses of metal. I've used the same 2mm-thick metal I use for chassis repairs for this bit, then slightly thinner metal for the other front-facing bit, which forms the edge of the A-pillar that the front panel wraps round. Get the basic shape of the thicker section first, then add the taper. I've used pen to mark the line I need to fold to. **03/04**

Seam weld it to the bottom of the pillar. Obviously, you will need to cut the step and inner valance away to properly repair the A-pillar, but you will almost certainly need to do this anyway. I've left some of the step in place to add extra strength to the area. **05**

Then add the second, thinner section. **06/07**

To finish the bottom of the pillar, make up something like this. **08**

Then weld to the bottom of the pillar. (A) is the external seam between the step and front panel with the A-pillar sandwiched

between them that you find on '68–'72 vans. **09**

This picture of the bottom of the A-pillar on the '79 shows how everything joins together. **10**

Inner valance

Late vans suffer from rot in the deformation panel and inner valance. The '79 had holes in the deformation panel for after-market indicators and looking through the hole it's obvious how much of the panel has rusted away. **11**

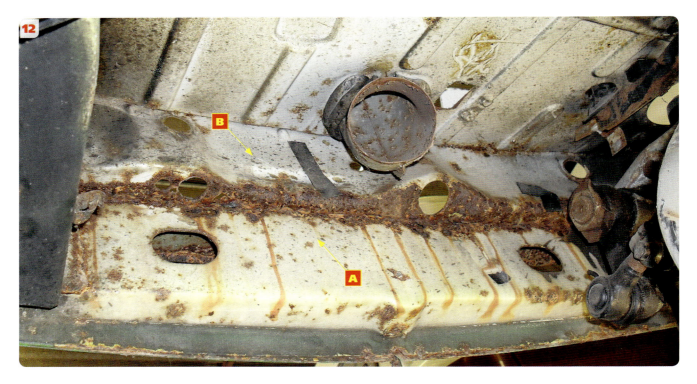

From underneath, the valance (A) and the washer bottle panel (B) are both holed. This area is particularly difficult to repair properly from underneath, which is why it's a common spot for bodges. **12**

As mentioned earlier, the change from early to late fronts was driven by safety legislation. The early valance is a double-skinned panel made of a thinner-gauge steel than the chassis. The late valance is thicker and stronger but is single skinned. However, much of the same information applies, you will probably still need to repair the A-pillars and possibly the end of the chassis legs. If you are replacing the inner valance and deformation panel on a late bay, remember that the genuine and repro deformation panels have the bumper holes aligned vertically for the Brazilian bays. You'll need to weld captive nuts in horizontally for original bumpers.

If you need to replace the inner valance, try to keep as much of the surrounding metal work in place as possible. If you cut the front arches, valance, cab floor and wheel housings away, there's not much left to hold the A-pillars in place and they will move, changing the shape of the door apertures and making it difficult to get the doors to fit. This is particularly the case if the doors and dash are still in place, adding extra weight.

When early vans were assembled, the valance was added in two parts, so the first part was spot-welded to the chassis and washer bottle panel, then the second part was spot-welded to that. You'll need to cut the outer part away to be able to get to the inner part to grind it away from the chassis legs. **13**

Drill out the line of spot-welds joining the valance to the washer bottle panel. **14**

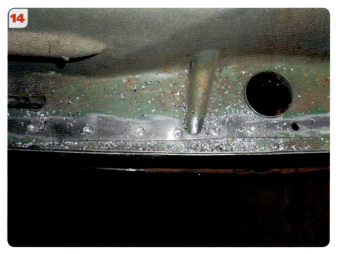

The repro inner valance comes with the two parts already joined together, so you need to weld the chassis to the valance from under the van. The valance was badly assembled. The outer section was lopsided so the valance wouldn't sit centrally. I ended up cutting and re-welding one end to make it meet the A-pillar.

The middle two chassis legs on early vans have a reinforcing plate on the front of each leg. Repair this if it needs attention and then drill it for plug-welding and spray with weld-through primer.

The more robust late valance welds straight to the front of the chassis legs. **15**

If the chassis legs need work, use the correct thickness of steel and always seam-weld repairs. It is possible to get a chassis repair kit for the outer legs, which comes in two sections, but

typically you'll have to repair further back into the area around the beam.

When the chassis legs and A-pillars are repaired, weld the new inner valance into place. I had to re-weld the bottom of the new valance because some of the spot-welds weren't holding the two layers of metal together. Always check the quality of the welds on cheaper repro panels. **16/17**

The inner part of the valance (A) extends to just past the outer chassis legs (B). You have to make up a section which joins the valance to the inside of the A-pillar (C). **18**

Front panel

Before you fit the front panel, clean up the A-pillars. You may need to repair the lip the panel wraps around if it is rusty and also the area near the bulge line, which often rusts through. Because the front panel only tacks to the A-pillars below the bulge you may as well give them a good coat of paint. Very little will burn off.

At the time of writing, the available front skins have a raised pressing for the

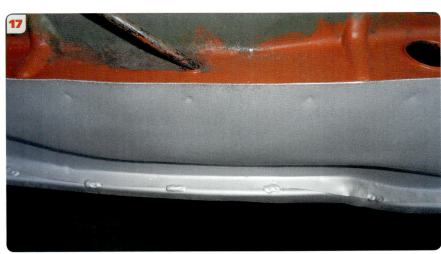

VW badge. Although it isn't a feature found on the original fronts, the smaller 73> VW badge fits on it perfectly, so you can leave the pressing in place. If you're converting to an early front, the bigger VW badge won't fit, so you'll need to remove the pressing and weld a new section of metal in. Do this before you fit the front panel. The air-box sits directly behind the pressing, making it impossible to seal the back of the panel after welding the new section in. **19**

I used the corresponding section of the old front to fill the hole. There is a slight curve in the panel here so it saves having to curve a piece of flat metal. There's about a 5mm overlap all the way round and I welded it from both sides. Finally, I painted and seam-sealed the rear. **20**

Prep the front panel and remember to drill holes in the top and sides of the air vent recess. Also put holes in the bottom of the air-box lip, which can then be plug-welded to the front panel. **21**

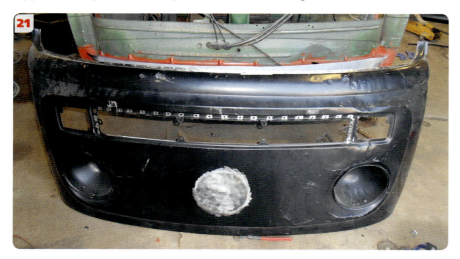

The final fitting of the front panel can be difficult. Make sure you've removed the remains of the old front from the air-box because any extra thickness of metal here will make fitting the panel at the A-pillars more difficult. There are several different methods for fitting the panel. Personally, I find it easiest to bend the lip on one edge past the 90 degrees it comes with. This allows you to hook that edge round the A-pillar without it slipping off. Then grip the headlight bowl and indicator recess and pull the other side over the A-pillar. **22**

Once you're happy with the fit of the panel, clamp it to the inner surround. You can then check the measurements for the windscreen aperture before plug-welding them together. The sections of the front panel above the bulge join the outer skin of the A-pillars. When fitting the new panel, cut it so that there is a slight overlap, then when you are happy with the position of the front panel, trim it down and butt-weld the join. Finish with a flap disk. **23**

Hammer the edges round the A-pillars while pressing a dolly against the front. Once you've started to bend them back on themselves, you can press them completely down using a pair of pump pliers. Use a thick (2mm+) piece of metal held against the front of the panel to ensure you don't mark the skin with the jaws. **24/25**

Up to this point, the process is more or less the same for early or late vans. If you are converting this panel for an early bay, you'll need to cut the bottom off the front skin where it joins to the inner valance (this was already done on this front skin) and use the repro lower front panel. Like many repro panels, the lower front is not a particularly good pressing. It extends to the bottom of the headlight bowls, but the pressing here is particularly bad so aim to join the panel around the indicators.

Offer the lower section up and clamp it in place against the inner valance. You can then work out roughly where to cut the two panels. You can overlap the panels or butt-weld them as I've done here, but allow a gap between the panels of 1mm and very slowly work your way across the front filling the gaps up. Whichever way you choose, seam-seal the join from inside the van. **26/27**

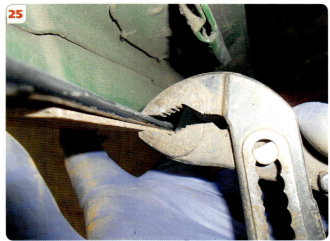

When you have finished, grind the welds down and finish with a flap wheel. Weld in the indicator sections from the old panel. You could do this before fitting the front, depending on where you decide to join the two parts of the front, but doing it after gives you a small degree of adjustment if you think the indicators look slightly lopsided. **28**

Make sure you get the cut-out sections the correct way up; the mounts that hold the indicator are not central. Check with an indicator body if you are unsure (A). Note that the lower front doesn't sit against the inner valance along its whole length, so make sure the plug-welding holes are in the correct places (B). **29**

These are the indicator blanking sections you need to use if your originals are too rusty. **30/31**

Screw the grill into place. Then use this to get the blanking plates correctly positioned, you need to make sure the gap between the grill and the front panel is the same all the way round.

I found I needed to trim the top and bottom of the blanks slightly to get them to sit inside the recess so they sat flush with the front panel. Weld them in slowly and finish with a flap disc. **32**

Weld the curve of the blanking panel to the front panel, then paint and seam-seal it. **33**

Once it is finished an early front conversion will need extra filler work around the panel joins, and the join